Enlightenment Through Entitlement

Enlightenment Through Entitlement

The **Root Cause** of All Stress, Guilt, Anxiety, Depression and Conflict in Mankind & The Newer Testament

The Messenger

Copyright © 2003 by *The Messenger*.

Edition One
Library of Congress Number: 2003098449
ISBN :   Hardcover   1-4134-3845-8
               Softcover   1-4134-3844-X

All rights reserved. No part of this book may be reproduced or transmitted in any form or by any means, electronic or mechanical, including photocopying, recording, or by any information storage and retrieval system, without permission in writing from the copyright owner.

This book was printed in the United States of America.

To order additional copies of this book, contact:
Xlibris Corporation
1-888-795-4274
www.Xlibris.com
Orders@Xlibris.com
18679

Contents

THE NEWER TESTAMENT 9

SECTION ONE - A MATTER OF ENERGY

DOORWAY ONE OF REALITY
   Teaching: In the beginning 15
DOORWAY TWO OF REALITY
   Teaching: Good News, Bad News 17
DOORWAY THREE OF REALITY
   Teaching: Hierarchy of Energy in People 27
DOORWAY FOUR OF REALITY
   Teaching: The "multi-categorical score-sheet" & Entitlement 38
DOORWAY FIVE OF REALITY
   Teaching: The Five Energy Tiers 43
DOORWAY SIX OF REALITY
   Teaching: The Medal Round 59

SECTION TWO - A MATTER OF INVISIBLE LAWS

DOORWAY SEVEN OF REALITY
   Teaching: The Golden Key and the Secret of Life 87
DOORWAY EIGHT OF REALITY
   Teaching: The Contrarian's View of Spirituality &
   The Philosophy of Human Energy Exchange 100

DOORWAY NINE OF REALITY
  Teaching: The Invisible Laws of reality 104
DOORWAY TEN OF REALITY
  Teaching: Revenge of the Narcissist,
  The Narcissistic Answer 108
DOORWAY ELEVEN OF REALITY
  Teaching: The Shawshank & Narcissist's Redemption 120
DOORWAY TWELVE OF REALITY
  Teaching: E=mc2 123
DOORWAY THIRTEEN OF REALITY
  Teaching: Perceptions 127
DOORWAY FOURTEEN OF REALITY
  Teaching: "The Multi-Categorical Score Sheet"
  inmore detail now 138
DOORWAY FIFTEEN OF REALITY
  Teaching: Stress, Anxiety, and Conflict are
  explainable and inevitable 147
DOORWAY SIXTEEN OF REALITY
  Teaching: Why at this time? 153

SECTION THREE - A MATTER OF SCIENCE

DOORWAY SEVENTEEN OF REALITY
  Teaching: The Trial of Reality 159
DOORWAY EIGHTEEN OF REALITY
  Teaching: Human Energy is finite 175
DOORWAYS NINETEEN THROUGH TWENTY-ONE
  Teaching: Right Now 178

SECTION FOUR - A MATTER OF REALITY

DOORWAY TWENTY-TWO OF REALITY
  Teaching: Thinking Poolside 181

DOORWAY TWENTY-THREE OF REALITY
Teaching: Discussion of Energy Class 184
DOORWAY TWENTY-FOUR OF REALITY
Teaching: More Details of the Score Chart 186
DOORWAY TWENTY-FIVE OF REALITY
Teaching: Stress from the Energy Loss/Gain Perspective 206
DOORWAY TWENTY-SIX OF REALITY
Teaching: Teaching: All Is Not One 209

SECTION FIVE - A MATTER OF NEUTRALITY

DOORWAY TWENTY-SEVEN OF REALITY
Teaching: Love, Law, "Free" Will, and "Neutral" Energy 217
DOORWAY TWENTY-EIGHT OF REALITY
Teaching: No such things as Coincidences & Accidents 223
DOORWAY TWENTY-NINE OF REALITY
Teaching: The Country Club 227
DOORWAY THIRTY OF REALITY
Teaching: Needs Versus Wants Explained 230
DOORWAY THIRTY-ONE OF REALITY
Teaching: Other Spiritual Teachers 232
DOORWAY THIRTY-TWO OF REALITY
Teaching: Some More Questions Answered 234
DOORWAY THIRTY-THREE OF REALITY
Teaching: Selflessness Does Not Exist 241
DOORWAY THIRTY-FOUR OF REALITY
Teaching: Use Your Intelligence 243
DOORWAY THIRTY-FIVE OF REALITY
Teaching: Yankee Stadium and Energy 245
DOORWAY THIRTY-SIX OF REALITY
Teaching: "Who knows what is good or bad?" 247

SECTION SIX - A MATTER OF EVOLUTION

DOORWAY THIRTY-SEVEN OF REALITY
   Teaching: Honestly speaking, how to get better and evolve *251*
DOORWAY THIRTY-EIGHT OF REALITY
   Teaching: How to feel better part two *257*
DOORWAY THIRTY-NINE OF REALITY
   Teaching: How to feel better part three *263*
DOORWAY FORTY OF REALITY
   Teaching: "Good" and "Evil" are the passwords that open up the doorway of War *272*
DOORWAY FORTY-ONE OF REALITY
   Teaching: Selfishness *276*
EPILOGUE 281
EPILOGUE CONTINUED
   Teaching: Free Flow Thoughts *286*

The Newer Testament

You are now at a point of no return, a point in time that you cannot resist. How can one achieve the very elusive *"Enlightenment"* through of all things *Entitlement*? Since when do these two words go together? Aren't they kind of like opposites? *Entitlement* is a "dirty" word and *Enlightenment* is such a "clean" word. Is this possibly what you were wondering before you picked up this book? A vortex in your life happens every second you are alive. A vortex is the collision of your subconscious, conscious, opportunity, preparation, and timing. The vortex is visible while the reasons behind it are mostly invisible. For example—look at any flag in the world. Their creations are vortexes. You see the visible manifestation of a certain nation's history, but you don't know all the reasons why the flag looks the way it does. They're stories and reasons behind every stripe, every star, and every color used on every flag in the world, it's just that you don't know the reasons why they exist the way they do. In the United States most people know the history behind our flag, but you'll be hard pressed to find someone who knows all the exact reasons behind why every other flag looks they way it does. Just because you don't know all the reasons for why something is the way it is obviously doesn't mean the reasons don't exist. They do. You just don't know what they are, that's all. All of life works the same way. The Universe has many invisible Laws at work that cause everything to manifest the way it does and this is what is now coming to light (and what this book is about).

The word "procrastination" or almost doing something, but not doing it, is almost a vortex except it misses one crucial element—timing. You want to do it and you just can't get yourself to do it so you postpone it for another time, for later. Well—it just wasn't the "time" to do it. It was "meant" for a later time when you were ready to do it. Anyway—the vortex of you picking up this book is simply a visible manifestation of you being ready to evolve into a higher state of consciousness. It is now your time that's all. After you read this book you will never be the same.

This book is about reality and how lives are lead in reality. People date each other as "test drives," but the illusion of let's date "just for fun" will always inevitably end as soon as one person cannot see a future with the other person. Why is this so? This is true because it is a waste of precious human energy (attention) to date someone if you are absolutely sure there is no future with him or her. What is needed in this situation for the couple to continue dating, seeing each other or to "picture a future" together? Both parties must believe that there will be the perceived ability to acquire a crude calculation of a perceived fair and equal exchange of human energy. Once one person **begins to think that there is not ENOUGH** "in it" for him or her, that person will move to end the relationship.

This book is a spiritual book and it should be made known upfront that even though I believe that the Universe/God is **ultimately neutral,** this does not mean I do not believe in the miracle of creation and all of life. As we all know, The Old and New Testament are filled with them (miracles that is), as are just about all scriptures in every known religion. The Big Bang theorists like myself still have to believe that "something" came from "nothing" and Darwinists must still believe in "leaps" and/or "the missing link" of evolution. Either way, however the Universe and mankind came into existence, something "miraculous" had to have occurred. This means something happened and we cannot explain how it occurred so we call it a "miracle." Invisible forces were at work. Anyway, as you will soon find out, the point of this book is not to answer the question of how the Universe started or how man came into being. The whole point of this book is to understand that whatever you believe, whatever camp you are in, your point of view has evolved inside you from a perspective of selfishness as Law #1 of this book explains:

Law #1—All human thought and action (including this book) has evolved to be one hundred percent defensive, protective, selfish, and self-serving so that one can avoid, relieve, reduce, or completely eliminate all forms of human suffering via a perceived equal and fair exchange of energy. Overall human energy balance (equilibrium) is what we seek and deserve. Human energy imbalance is the *root cause* of all conceivable forms of human suffering and all so called *"mental illnesses."*

Question: Doesn't the word miracle imply a "good" God or Universe?

Answer: No it does not. A miracle is just a vortex happening without you knowing all the reasons why the event happened. As stated, just because you don't know all the reasons why something has occurred doesn't mean they don't exist. We just call inexplicable events "miracles" that's all. A so-called miracle therefore does not imply "good" or "evil"—it is just a *neutral event* happening that is extremely improbable, seemingly impossible, or at the very least very hard to explain how the event in question occurred at all in the first place. Let's look at two quick examples of "miraculous" vortexes:

A "good or bad miracle" is in the eyes of the beholder:

1. Ask any Boston Red Sox fan about Game Six of the 1986 World Series and then ask any New York Mets fan about the same game.
2. Ask any fan of the 1980 USA Men's Olympic Ice Hockey Team about the game against the Soviet Union and then ask any Soviet Union Hockey Team fan about the same exact game.

In both these cases, many fans rooting for the winning side deemed the miraculous victories as "good" while the fans on the losing heartbreak side viewed these games as miraculous "loses" or "bad" events in their lives. In the long run everything is *ultimately neutral* including all miracles. The fact that miracles have happened (the creation of the Universe and mankind) does not mean it is a "good" Universe or a "good" God at work. Until it is proven (and it never will be) that the Creator has a personality and cares one way or another about anything here on earth, it is much more sensible and logical to believe in *the ultimate neutrality* of the Universe and all assignments/events/vortexes played out here on earth as being neutral. It is your selfish perception as it relates to you and your well being whether or not the external or internal event/miracle is "good" or not.

Since this book is about *reality* I will start you off with this: You will cry when the vortex for you to cry is upon you, you will live or die when the vortex of living or dying is upon you, you will read this book when the vortex for reading this book is upon you. In short, you will do what your body tells you to do, you will speak your truth when it is your vortex to do so, and you will evolve when you are also meant to do so. You must read this book with this in mind: Your life is an *ultimately impersonal, ultimately impartial*, and an *ultimately neutral experience*. Since it is now clear that "good" or "bad" doesn't universally exist in *reality* what is left? The only thing left to do is what has always been the only thing actually happening—evolution. It is now time for the evolution of consciousness, as we will now rise to higher states of *awareness of reality*. Happy reading and happy evolving because that's all there is to do, as this book also is *ultimately neutral*.

SECTION ONE

A Matter Of Energy

Doorway One of reality

Teaching: In the beginning

Dear Reader,

Before you begin your walk through the doorways of *reality* an oath is in order. Sail away with me to another world—this world.

The Silent Majority's Oath of Reality

I, *state your name*, on this date *state today's date* understand that as a human being I am a selfish creature. I bought or otherwise have this book in my possession because I hope to avoid, reduce, relieve, or altogether eliminate all forms of conceivable human suffering as they pertain to me first and foremost. While it is true that I wish no harm on my fellow man and hope only for "good" things ("good" is in the eyes of the beholder) as the human species continues to evolve, I must always remember that my feeling of overall well-being comes first. As I attempt to make myself as peaceful as possible, I am fully aware that I may have to hurt other human beings in the process as we compete and fight with one another for scarce finite human energy. There simply isn't enough to go around. In general, the more threatened my overall wellness becomes, the more selfish and aggressive I will become. The word "selfish" does not connote a pejorative meaning in my *ultimately neutral* view of *reality*. It is what it is—*neutral reality*. *Reality* is not something that can be removed or transcended, as all attempts to do so will inevitably prove futile. My overall peace of mind and wellness is my first priority and I am not ashamed to admit this truth. I believe there is nothing wrong with being a selfish, self-interested human being because all human beings are, and it is simply the true nature of *reality*. I understand many people on planet earth are blind to this truth, but I am not one of them. All other human beings who do not admit to being selfish are either knowing liars or unaware of the true nature of *reality*. Everything written in these pages will appear somewhat familiar to me because it's everything I already know about *reality* except was afraid to say. Amen.

Doorway Two of reality

Teaching: Good News, Bad News

Hello reader and welcome home to the *new leader in reality*. Psychotherapy, psychiatry, philosophy, sociology, and spirituality have completely missed the boat with regards to *reality*, and the worldwide view of *reality* will now (by virtue of what you are about to read) be re-evaluated. To be quite frank, people are starving for a dose of *reality* because nobody, until now, has stepped up to the plate and explained things *as they actually are*. Inventing theories of *reality* should in fact be a business. We live in a capitalistic society and this book welcomes its future competition into this new marketplace. It is only through competition that improvements can and will be made to the *theory of reality*. Let the people decide who has it right and who doesn't. I welcome all future debates about this extraordinary topic. I can't wait to debate you! This book is the closest possible explanation of *reality* currently in print. It takes courage to read a book like this, but since I've captured your attention (your energy), I would like to offer you one thing—*this book will be a perceived equal and fair exchange of energy* for you as you begin to learn and understand the *theory of reality*. I guarantee it. The world has been waiting for this book. Its creation was inevitable since the human being species is an always-evolving one and evolution of consciousness is what being a human being is all about. This book represents the much-anticipated awakening of the collective subconscious.

17

"Good" News and "Bad" News

Theory of Reality, Pride & Entitlement

The Good News

Question: What's the good news?
Answer: The "good" news is that human beings, although one hundred percent selfish, are a fair and equal minded species. In other words, we only want what we feel *entitled* to. If we get more than we deserve or feel *entitled* to, *we feel guilty* and have an instinctual need *to find equilibrium* (balance) once again. In other words, we take, take, take, until we get what we feel we deserve in life. Once we reach our *entitlement* point (what we feel we deserve), we don't have the desire to take anymore. If we get more than we feel *entitled* to (and consequently *feel guilty*), we actually have the instinctual desire to "give back" human energy so that we can selfishly feel best about ourselves. The *root motivation is always selfishness in order to feel "good."* The whole trick is this: A *"fair" or "equal" exchange is in the eyes of the beholder and entitlement for a certain amount of energy is the secret invisible energy force controlling every human inter-action.*

The Bad News

Question: What is the *root cause* of all stress and conflict in mankind? What's the bad news?
Answer: When two or more human beings feel *entitled* to the same exact thing.
Question: What is that "same exact thing?"
Answer: *Control* of *equilibrium energy on demand.* This constant fight is over who will lose their *control of*

equilibrium energy on demand (pride, people, ambiance, or money energy etc.) and who will not in such a battle. In other words—who ends up "superior" to who and why and who ends up "beneath" whom and why. The battle is quite simply over *pride, entitlement, and most often money energy.* In plain English, this crazy world is all about the constant fight over what is acceptable to each human being's sense of *pride* over where they perceive they fit in with regards to the overall hierarchy of life. **People subconsciously demand a perceived fair and equal exchange for who they perceive they are.**

Question: Why is this "bad" news?

Answer: This is the exhausting nature of reality as people are constantly sizing each other up to see where they fit in on the "hierarchy of life" and it makes for a constant litigious (argumentative) planet. It is not made up in your mind if someone gives off the aura that they feel they are "better" or "superior" to you. It is a real thing happening in our daily lives to all of us all of the time and is part of the *true nature of reality*. There is nothing we can do about it except to own up to the fact that it is simply part of *reality* here on planet earth. Each person wants *and feels entitled to* the vibration or frequency of life that they feel they deserve and will subtly send off signals to show the person below them (usually with utmost "politeness" and "consideration") who is in charge of whom. Those below try to rise up and go higher only to find their rightful place in the "hierarchical structure" of life as their nervous system (and other human systems) gets conditioned to what feels most comfortable to them. **All is not one** and any spiritual teacher who claims this is terribly mistaken. *Ultimately* nothing matters, but while we are all here competing, *it all does*. Other spiritual teachers miss the dynamic of time—our time

on planet earth. **Your life is only personal to you as it is an impersonal energy supply to others who interact and live around you.** You are just an object, a tool, and a pawn so that others can get what they want from you—your human energy. As you go through life, you will see how your energy affects others around you and their well being as it relates to them having you in their life or not. Your well—being is only personal to you and even that is *ultimately impersonal* because we all know we will die one day. When we die—we simply release back our energy to the Universe (where it came from originally). The energy we released in our life-spans (such as me releasing this book—stay forever). Even if this book were to be destroyed permanently—it would live on if one person reads it. Then it will have some influence over that person's viewpoint of life and they will then transfer this new energy form all around (certain thoughts about life etc). This is what I have done here, all this energy came into me and I reconfigured it and released it back out to the Universe/Society. Energy in = Energy out. Everything we do or say in life is exactly what it appears to be (one hundred percent selfish) though people often claim it is not their true intention (to be selfish). People who claim to be altruistic or selfless are simply unaware human beings. The truth is that life is for fighting and for wars; it's that simple. **Entitlement** is the dynamic that determines who gets what and why (see multi-categorical score-sheet teaching later on). The time dynamic is often forgotten about when other spiritual teachers talk, and it should be made known that while we are alive here on earth that the hierarchical structure is *very real and very brutal.* Being materialistic, *feeling entitled* to nice things, believing in a hierarchical structure to reality, and selfishness does not mean one need not be spiritual. *The two are not mutually exclusive.* You can be a so-called "arrogant snob" and be a very spiritual person all at the same time. The idea that *enlightenment and entitlement* could go together is indeed revolutionary. The word *enlightenment* just means awareness so become aware of what *entitlement* is, that's all. Keep reading.

It's all about energy

All forms of energy (except one) are scarce, finite, *ultimately* impersonal, *ultimately* impartial, and *ultimately* neutral. *Divine (God/Universe/Creator/Higher Power) energy* is the only form that is not scarce or finite, but it too is *ultimately* impersonal, *ultimately* impartial, and *ultimately* neutral. God does not take sides, play favorites, or play dice. This teacher believes in *A Neutral Universe or A Neutral God. The invisible LAWS of reality have now finally been discovered and are presented in these writings for the world to read and test in their own lives.*

Question: Are all energy forms created equal?
Answer: No. As you will latter understand there are energy tiers and the GOLD MEDAL goes to *"aware with peace of mind energy"* (the most valuable and hardest to find).

Cut to the chase

Question: Is there "good," "evil," "right," or "wrong?"
Answer: "Right, good, evil, and wrong" with regards to morality do not exist. Right with regards to "true" or "correct" does exist and so does wrong when it means "false" or "incorrect." A true or false answer means a very different thing from a "right" or "wrong" answer with regards to morality on planet earth. Understanding this difference is job number one. Basically the words

"true" and "false" are reserved only for such fields as math and science. Morality is a man made invention.

Question: Why is this? Isn't God the *ultimate* judge?

Answer: God is *neutral energy* and *neutral energy* is God. God is *ultimately* neutral, *ultimately* impersonal, and *ultimately* impartial. He/She/It will judge nothing. In plain English, God/Universe/Whatever you want to call it set in motion visible laws (which we already know a lot about) and the *invisible laws* of the **human energy world** that we must live by (which we are discovering now in these writings). It is the invisible laws that we are concerned with in these revolutionary writings. In short, *this book is bringing to light all the invisible laws of the Universe.*

Question: What about positive, negative, and neutral energy?

Answer: This is all how you perceive the energy in your environment and your overall life. *It's in the eyes of the beholder and how we filter it.* Whatever feels "good" to us or aids our ability to survive is called "positive energy" and whatever hinders our ability to survive we call "negative" energy. Note—if you get more energy than you feel ENTITLED TO, you will feel guilty and a need to give back. Therefore too little energy or not a fair exchange (too much energy) is "negative" or "energy leakage" or "energy implosion." A perceived equal and fair exchange feels "good" so we call that "positive energy." "Positive energy" simply means we are in balance with getting what we feel entitled to. The whole idea of this game (the game of planet earth) is to find equilibrium energy WHICH WE CALL "POSITIVE ENERGY" because it feels "good" to us and aids our ability to survive. All the energy is neutral around us but we filter it and perceive it in ways by virtue of the way it makes our body feel. The tricky part is this: too much energy or more than one feels entitled *to causes suffering so we call that guilt which also has the side effect of being called "negative energy."*

Nature versus Nurture

If we open our eyes to *reality* we see that we are the way we are due to **SOCIETAL NURTURING.** This means and encompasses everything about us. Whatever we look like and how we behave is a product of our conditioned nervous system and all human energy systems each day, each moment we are alive. Whoever raised us (usually our parents) had many years of conditioning us and telling us how to think, what to do, what not to touch etc. Society conditioning or nurturing is the combination of nature and nurture working in tandem. To keep this simple— just pretend society raised you and responded to what you looked like. Once our karmic trajectory was/is in place, off we go into society as young adults with our previously conditioned responses to external events. The programming never ends. It's always a one thing leads to another model of reality with selfishness being the backbone, the foundation to all thought and to all action.

Let's start at the beginning of a new day. We wake up and we feel *agitation energy* (stress/nervous/ambivalence energy) that empowers us to do things we do so that we can relieve, avoid, reduce, or completely eliminate the *agitation energy* (suffering) we had to begin with. Some of the feelings we have during the day are pleasure and pain, love and hate, ambition, desire, inspiration, boredom and laziness etc. Our feelings go up and down like a crazy roller coaster as the stimuli of the external world gets internalized within our perceptions of what the external stimuli means or doesn't mean to our perception of what creates or doesn't create suffering within us. The explanation of why different minds feel different things at different times is quite simple to explain *in reality*. *In reality*, the law of cause and effect reigns supreme, which is the theory of karma in Buddhist teachings. The theory of karma has never been explained this way however. Forget the nonsense of past lives and future lives and just focus on this life. In this life our instinct (genetics) and all our "human systems" get conditioned once we are here (born) by real life experiences. The nervous system is the main system that controls what we do, but all the "human energy systems" can and do get conditioned. As we begin to understand that there is an inherent hierarchical structure in reality—we learn where we fit in by **SOCIETAL NURTURING. In other words, this means, how society accepts us and on what terms. Basically we find out what we can get away with and what we cannot.** We live our lives in a one thing leads to another trajectory as we try and makes ourselves feel "less bad" or "most good" every step of the way. Every human being is doing the same exact thing except on different vibration/frequency/energy levels in the hierarchy of life (more on this later).

This is the only difference among us.

The frequency or energy level you live on could in fact be higher, the same, or lower, than another human being at this particular time. *The frequency is always changing as the karmic wheel of fate is always spinning.* This is because we were all born with different amounts of energy (genetics, lineage etc.) and our conditioning may be more or less "expensive" than another. In other words, some of us got used to "expensive things" while others got used to "cheaper things." Some of us got more attention growing up based on our looks and currently consider ourselves better looking than others around us. There is a truth to beauty; it is not just an opinion or belief. The human energy marketplace determines who has beauty and who does not. Of course there is a huge gray area, but most of the people most of the time will agree who has "beauty or sex energy" and who does not (especially on the extreme polar opposites of beautiful and ugly). Beauty or sex energy is in fact valuable in the eyes of society and that is that. Once again and to be clear, we must acknowledge that there is a huge gray area in between, but overall most people will agree most of the time who is good looking and who is not. There is a ranking, a hierarchy of people based on many categories (multi-categorical score-sheet) that do or do not emanate energy fields. Your selfish conditioned human energy systems pick up on the energy fields that feel best for it to do so. We end up liking only what feels like an *overall crude calculation of human energy equilibrium (overall summation of the energy exchange between two people)*. Physical attractiveness is clearly a category that matters to many people on planet earth. We must acknowledge that some people on planet earth seemingly couldn't care less what some someone looks like (but rank and judge other things about the person) so that is that. Everyone wants an *overall crude calculation of human energy equilibrium* in life.  People who are blind to this truth (that everything is ranked) are simply defending themselves and their lifestyles to make themselves feel the best they can about themselves or the least bad about themselves. Once again, that is that. We must always remember though, everything is a defense **and I mean everything** (every word, action, or thought) is a defense against life. This book is my defense as I fight my personal, yet *ultimately* impersonal battle with life. To all the people who counted on me to be passive and surrender, you counted wrong. The Gods of War have been awoken within me and I fight this war because that is all there is—a war for the sake of a war over human energy. It is now time for *The Messenger* to speak, as he can no longer silently tolerate the current nonsensical worldview of *reality*.

Question: What the hell we fighting for? Countdown to reality 3, 2, 1-zero
Answer: It's a constant fight for Energy. Human Energy.
Question: Why is this so obvious to me and seemingly no one else?
Answer: I no longer care why or how this gift came upon me, but it did so I'll write a book about it. Buy it or not, I don't really care. What you are reading is how I, a certain human energy system, a certain stranger to you, a certain fellow traveler on this planet, see things in this world.

Some definitions

Energy

Energy is the ability to do ***work*** or ***produce change***. There is only one kind of energy, but it may exist in many forms including potential, kinetic, electrical, strain, chemical, internal, and heat. No matter in what form the energy exists; energy is a product of the force on a body and the distance over which the energy is exerted. [E=Fxd] Work is a form of energy.

Any system or machine gives back exactly the same amount of energy put into it. Some energy may be used for work, while other energy may be wasted as heat or stored as potential energy.

Human Energy

Human energy is used when we pay attention to anything, have internal perceptions, or do physical labor of any kind. Humans are not one hundred percent efficient so some work done (energy) is lost. In the world of physics this is called friction. This lost work (energy) **is human emotion and moods** (feeling just okay, better, or worse). There are simple humans and very complex humans just as there are simple machines and very complex ones.

Mass

Mass is the amount of material in an object (condensed energy). Mass differs from volume which is the amount of space an object takes up. Mass also differs from weight. Weight is a force. For example, a person who weighs 100 pounds on earth will weigh less on the moon due to the decreased gravitational force. This person will have the same amount of mass no matter if on the moon or earth.

Doorway Three of reality

Teaching: Hierarchy of Energy in People

Hierarchy Time

Question: Is there a hierarchical structure to mankind or are all people created equal?
Answer: The world is kind of like a constantly moving and changing caste system dynamic. You can change caste on a moment-to-moment basis. For example—if you feel very attractive for an evening out, or if you make a lot of money on a certain day etc. you will feel the energy gain. As you will soon learn, this text refers to always moving and changing *"energy class"* which historically is most similar to the old Hindu caste system. The old Hindu caste system is just *a good starting point for reality* learning, *but it is not* **reality**. **Reality is based on the "multi-categorical" scoresheet (which is coming a bit later on).**

History

The Hindu caste system is comparable to class structures in other countries, except that this Indian system has been rigidly enforced and has lasted for two or three thousand years. The caste system was enforced as law throughout the subcontinent

27

until the adoption of the Indian constitution in 1949, which outlawed the caste system. However, it remains a deeply ingrained social structure, particularly in rural India.

There are four main castes into which everyone was categorized. At the very top were the *Brahmins*—the priests, scholars, and philosophers. The second highest caste was the *Kshatriyas*. These were the warriors, rulers, and those concerned with the defense and administration of the village or state. Third came the *Vaishyas*, who were traders, merchants, and people involved in agricultural production. The lowest caste was the *Shudras*—the laborers and servants for the other castes. Each caste included many hierarchical subcastes divided by occupation.

Below even the *Shudras* were the Untouchables. These people had no caste at all. They performed the most menial of jobs, such as dealing with dead bodies and cleaning toilets. Higher-caste people believed that if they touched one of the caste-less, they would be contaminated and would need to go through cleansing rituals.

Caste was determined by birth—you fell into the same caste as your parents, and there was almost no way to change it. The caste system dictated your occupation, choice of spouse, and many other aspects of your life. If you did something outside your caste, you could be excommunicated from your caste. That would cut you off from doing any work to support yourself because you could only do the jobs allowed by your caste.

Today, features of the caste system linger throughout Indian society. Laws prohibit discrimination based on caste, and the government runs affirmative action programs for lower castes, especially the Untouchables (now called *Dalits*). But caste continues to play a part in marriages, and some politicians actually campaign for caste-based votes. Maybe the system will change more dramatically in this new millennium.

Intimate/Romantic Relationships

When people look to form partnerships with other people (otherwise known as relationships), people do in fact in ***reality*** "comparison shop" people with other people as if they were impersonal products on a shelf (initially). ***People are constantly searching for a perceived fair exchange of their energy.*** In other words, they compare themselves to others, figure out where they fit in on the hierarchy and look for **human energy equilibrium** with their partner. If a person over-steps or under-steps where they fit in on the hierarchy, they will feel the pain caused by *energy imbalance syndrome* and a breakup will be inevitable. *Energy imbalance syndrome* is as the title of this book suggests The *Root Cause* of All Stress, Guilt, Anxiety, Depression and Conflict in Mankind.

Getting Acquainted With Reality

Ok time to learn about the "multi-categorical" score-sheet. I will now attempt to ease you into the thinking of the silent vast majority. The type of thinking I am about to bring to light should not come as a surprise to you. It's what you already know about *reality* except it's lodged deep in your subconscious. It is now time for some conscious awareness of *reality*.

Introducing the "Multi-categorical score-sheet" of energy forms that emanate directly or indirectly from human beings.

Perception is reality

It is all in my (your) perception, but *perception is reality*.
There are many forms of energy in the Universe. Here is a good look at most of them. There are all the energy forms that come from people (like 200 forms), the five tiers of energy that come everywhere and anywhere, and the energy currency that humans use in order to get all the other forms of energy (attention, internal perceptions, and physical work or labor). To keep this simple at this stage just look at your attention as your energy. Wherever your attention goes, your energy goes. It is with this currency—your attention that you seek a

perceived equal and fair return for your energy investment (your attention). The energy list is infinite in theory with regards to the Universe, but it is finite here on earth (we know we will die as our lives have timelines). After you get the idea of what energy forms look like, we will then focus in detail together on some of the forms. I will then teach to you what I believe to be the top three most valuable forms.

MANY OF THE CATEGORIES ARE HERE

Invisible or Must Ask The Person in Question	Visible or Need Not Ask The Person in Question
Family Tree	Physical Strength
Heritage	Physical Health
Birthright	Fitness
Inheritance	Sex (male or female)
Tradition	Race
Genetics/DNA	Reflexes
Intelligence	Laugh
IQ	Voice
*Powerful Last Name	*Powerful Last Name
*Hero/Celebrity/Fame Status	*Hero/Celebrity/Fame Status
Social Breeding	Smell
Social Affiliations	Vision
Professional Affiliations	Height
Creativity	Weight
Hobbies	Body Shape
Appreciation of Arts	Smooth Skin Face
Lifestyle	Smooth Skin Back
Attitude	Smooth Skin Chest
Spirituality	Smooth Skin Arms
Awareness	Smooth Skin Legs
Religion	Hair
Peer Group	Eye Color
Address Raised	Eye Shape
Atmosphere Raised	Eyebrows
Address Present	Eyelashes

Enlightenment Through Entitlement | 31

Ability to "roll with punches" in life	Eyelids
Ability to "Function"	Eye Socket (bags etc).
Education Level	Nose Shape
Education (Schools Attended)	Nostrils
Credentials	Ears
Ambition	Ear Lobes
Wealth	Upper Lip
Work Ethic	Lower Lip
Income	Face
Socio-Economic Class	Lack of Wrinkles
Social Status	Cheekbones
Net Worth	Chin
Well Written	Head
Well Spoken	Forehead
Well Read	Arms
Charm	Elbows
Confidence	Forearms
Perceptiveness	Hands
Intuition	Palms
Grace	Fingers
Rhythm	Fingernails
Coordination	Knuckles
Manners	Shoulders
Refinement	Cleavage
Sophistication	Chest
Book Smarts	Breasts
Street Smarts	Nipples
Regal Etiquette	Stomach
Athletic Ability	Lack of or not, Body Hair (upper body)
Birthplace	Lack of or not, Body Hair (lower body)
Zodiac Sign	Lack of or not, Body Hair (back)
Multi-Cultural Knowledge	Lack of or not, Facial Hair
Humor	Upper Back
Personality	Lower Back
Expertise	Body Type
Personal Accomplishments	Accent
Specialized Knowledge	Waist
Occupational Status	Hips
Desired Occupational Status	Skin Tone

Basic Common Knowledge	Belly Button
Nationality	Love Handles
Style (clothes, hair etc)	Inner Thigh
Taste	Outer Thigh
Personal Habits	Legs
Personal Hygiene	Knees
World Travels	Shins
Popularity	Feet
Pride	Sole Feet
Charisma	Toes
Metabolism	Toenails
Sexual Orientation	Lack of or not visible veins
Actual Life Experiences	Neck
Chronological Age	Décolleté
Physical Age	Calves
Psychological Age	Ankles
Spiritual Age	Tongue
Aptitude to learn new things	Genitalia Shape
Desires	Genitalia Size
Cravings	Genitalia Functionality
Physical Needs	Genitalia Pride
Physical Space Needs	Seductiveness
Privacy Needs	Sexual Abilities
Intellectual Strength	Teeth
Mental Strength	Gums
Emotional Strength	Smile
Interesting Personality (Engaging Conversationalist)	Adam's Apple
Prior Nervous System Conditioning	Wrists
Religious Thoughts	Flexibility
Political Thoughts	Masculine
Social Thoughts	Feminine
Sexual Thoughts	Buttocks
Family Values	Dimples
Self-Esteem	Lack of or not beauty marks
Social Skills	Walk
Parental Abilities	Stance
Entitlement for nice things	Posture
Lack of or not Powerful Aura/Energy field	Presentation, Packaging, Overall Look
Body Attitude	Lack of or not Blemishes

ENLIGHTENMENT THROUGH ENTITLEMENT | 33

Outlook on Life	Tattoos/Body Art
Employment Stability	Body Piercing
ADD WHATEVER YOU	FEEL IS IMPORTANT

* *Powerful Last Name/Hero/Celebrity/Fame Status is something you previously may or may not know about someone. They may come from a famous family or be a celebrity etc., but you may not have heard of them that's all.*

Teaching: THE ENERGY STANDARD

The way this works is the total internal perception of oneself is derived from the summation of every single category in the soon to be discussed score-sheet, and the weighted perceived importance of each category with regards to acquiring the most human energy possible from *the theoretical "range of standard energy desirability."* The theory states: the *"range of standard energy desirability"* is the *"energy standard."* Once we feel *safe*, we aim to acquire the *energy standard*. Technically, human energy is mental work and/or physical work. For the purposes of this book we assume that any physical work requires mental work on some level (subconscious etc.). Therefore from here on out, the term "human energy" means the E and the m—*attention and/or internal perceptions, and attention and/or internal perceptions means human energy.*

* *The theoretical range of standard energy desirability = energy standard*

Question: What is the *theoretical range of standard energy desirability and why is it the energy standard?*

Answer: At first thought, the highest vibration (vibe), aura, or energy (the word I will be using) in mankind would appear to emanate from an extremely attractive king or queen whose royal lineage is infinite (from the beginning of time to end of time). This is not true. The *energy standard* in mankind in theory comes from Mr. and Mrs./Ms. *"theoretical range of standard energy desirability."* This means it is not from a king or queen. This range is the theoretical weighted average of all of society's human energy. In other words, the human energy from the highest combination of *perceived quality and perceived quantity.* If only extremely attractive kings and queens were to pay attention and/or have high internal perceptions of you, this would only equal a few people on earth if any. On the other hand, if only extremely unattractive peasants (of infinite peasant lineage) give you their human energy, this would include millions of people *(quantity),* but with a very low grade with regards to *quality* of energy. The trick then is to attain the energy standard—the hypothetical *"range of standard energy desirability."* In business terms, one could do sensitivity analysis and find the point where *quality and quantity intersect* at the highest possible point on the graph. People in business know that there's an inverse relationship to price and volume. This is the same relationship with regards to the type of energy we speak of. The quality of energy is the price, and the higher the price (kings and queens), the less the volume (fewer people). In other words, an extremely attractive king or queen with infinite lineage would have the highest price, but none if any exist.

Here is my opinion on the matter in a more simplified way:

Energy Price	Theoretical Energy Class
100	Extremely Attractive King/Queen (of infinite lineage)
75	¾ class
50	Average person
25	¼ class
0	Extremely Unattractive Peasants (of infinite lineage)

Chameleon Time

The Energy Standard Teaching Continued

In my perception, the energy standard (*theoretical range of standard energy desirability*) would be in the 70-80 range. Each person may have a different perspective on the matter. Some may think, the "average person" is this magical spot (50), others may think it's the "ever so slightly above average" person (51). My perspective is that "significantly above average," but not "too significantly above average" is where the *theoretical range of standard energy desirability* (energy standard) is hiding. It is better to use the word range than point because an exact science my teachings are not. This is why *it is a theory*. All religions, spiritual thought, and psychiatry are based on theories and none of them are scientifically provable. It is my belief that my theories are in fact *less outlandish and more provable because I have laws of physics on my side. Yes some Science—the Science of energy movement is on my side and is in AN ENTIRE SECTION of this book (a little latter on we have a physics class). The premise is simple—human beings are energy balancing machines.*

Back to the teachings:

The 70-80 range person could still relate to the masses, the spiritual leaders, *and also the kings and queens of the world*. A 51 person (in my perspective) wouldn't feel comfortable around Kings and Queens, and therefore would never receive their *very valuable* energy. It is simply my perspective that the "70-80" people are the proper range for the *range of standard energy desirability (energy standard)*. As stated, the theory put forth allows for different perspectives on this tricky matter. For the remainder of this text we will simply refer to this as *"the energy standard."*

The Multi-Categorical Score Sheet of Hybrid Energy Forms

People will inevitably disagree on which categories get the "energy standard's" human energy (most people agree that attractiveness is important). People will perceive that certain categories are more important than others, but either way, we are all mixtures or blends of everything that we are in these categories.

We must always keep in mind that every millimeter (whatever the smallest unit of measure is) of your physical body is ranked. People such as face, hand, feet, and teeth models do exist *and get paid*. There is a market rate (meaning money), for some physical features and not for others. Different people prefer different physical attributes. This is why some guys walk around saying they are an "ass" man etc. These men (or women) are very unenlightened because they only go by one, two, or few categories. If they read this book however, *awareness of reality* is possible. In reality—energy emanates from every part of your physical being but there are not specific models for everything. We judge the "whole package." Back to models for a second: In fact, the more valuable the model's physical attribute, the more likely he or she will have an insurance policy protecting against the loss of their particular asset.

Examples of physical features are smile, laugh, accent, voice, hair, flexibility, coordination, grace, posture, stamina, smell, breath, snore etc. etc. The list is infinite and is up to each person's conditioned nervous system to determine which feature(s) gives off energy and which ones do not. Remember about what I said before the Big Bang—internal perceptions are infinite *relative to the Universe. Relative to humans and planet earth, they are finite.*

Energy on planet earth is scarce and finite, and it makes sense that high paid models would want to protect what they've got (why they have insurance covering the physical attribute they have). In other words a hand model will have an insurance policy on their hand (this is how they make a living).

Non-Physical (invisible) categories are ranked the same way. Once again the categories are infinite as is up to each person's conditioned *nervous/human systems* to determine which feature(s) give off energy and which ones do not. Examples include: IQ, lineage, birthright, heritage, tradition, breeding, intelligence, personality, legacy, manners, zodiac sign, birthplace, address raised, income, potential income, power etc. etc.

The fact that **everything** is ranked in a hierarchical structure should not come as a surprise to you. There are attractive peasants, ugly Kings and okay looking Queens etc. The trick of life is to find out and to accept where you fit in. Everybody initially shoots for the top (the highest they believe they can go), but then his or her nervous system (and all human systems) rights the course into his or her unique vibration/frequency level (reality).

Doorway Four of reality

Teaching: The "multi-categorical score-sheet" & Entitlement

Example of a "multi-categorical" score sheet

This is the theory (3 steps)

Step 1 = Column 2 X Column 3 = Column 4
Step 2 = Add up all the numbers in Column 4
Step 3 = If you do this with a friend, use same exact categories to find out who feels more entitled to more human energy in life.

		Column 2	Column 3	Column 4
	Self-Perception	Rank Yourself	How Important is Category Weigh the Categories	Your Energy Class
	CATEGORIES	In what % (percentile) of society are you in 1 – 100 % 1 is the worst 100 is the best	In your internal perception how much ATTENTION do you receive from *THE ENERGY STANDARD? The Energy Standard is Defined Above One Through Infinity	Entitlement Feelings for market rate for "human energy" Summation of this column is YOUR ENTITLEMENT FOR HUMAN ENERGY
1	Family Tree	85	1000	85000
2	Heritage		Etc.	So on and so forth

38

Enlightenment Through Entitlement | 39

3	Birthright	Etc.	So on and so forth
4	Inheritance		
5	Tradition		
6	Genetics/DNA		
7	Intelligence		
8	IQ		
9	*Powerful Last Name		
10	*Hero/Celebrity/Fame Status		
11	Social Breeding		
12	Social Affiliations		
13	Professional Affiliations		
14	Creativity		
15	Hobbies		
16	Appreciation of Arts		
17	Lifestyle		
18	Attitude		
19	Spirituality		
20	Awareness		
21	Religion		
22	Peer Group		
23	Address Raised		
24	Atmosphere Raised		
25	Address Present		
26	Ability to "roll with punches" in life		
27	Ability to "Function"		
28	Education Level		
29	Education (Schools Attended)		
30	Credentials		
31	Ambition		
32	Wealth		
33	Work Ethic		
34	Income		
35	Socio-Economic Class		
36	Social Status		
37	Net Worth		
38	Well Written		
39	Well Spoken		
40	Well Read		
41	Charm		
42	Confidence		
43	Perceptiveness		
44	Intuition		
45	Grace		
46	Rhythm		
47	Coordination		
48	Manners		
49	Refinement		
50	Sophistication		
51	Book Smarts		
52	Street Smarts		
53	Regal Etiquette		
54	Athletic Ability		
55	Birthplace		
56	Zodiac Sign		
57	Multi-Cultural Knowledge		
58	Humor		
59	Personality		
60	Expertise		
61	Personal Accomplishments		
62	Specialized Knowledge		
63	Occupational Status		

64	Desired Occupational Status		
65	Basic Common Knowledge		
66	Nationality		
67	Style (clothes, hair etc)		
68	Taste		
69	Personal Habits		
70	Personal Hygiene		
71	World Travels		
72	Popularity		
73	Pride		
74	Charisma		
75	Metabolism		
76	Sexual Orientation		
77	Actual Life Experiences		
78	Chronological Age		
79	Physical Age		
80	Psychological Age		
81	Spiritual Age		
82	Aptitude to learn new things		
83	Desires		
84	Cravings		
85	Physical Needs		
86	Physical Space Needs		
87	Privacy Needs		
88	Intellectual Strength		
89	Mental Strength		
90	Emotional Strength		
91	Interesting Personality (Engaging Conversationalist)		
92	Prior Nervous System Conditioning		
93	Religious Thoughts		
94	Political Thoughts		
95	Social Thoughts		
96	Sexual Thoughts		
97	Family Values		
98	Self-Esteem		
99	Social Status		
100	Parental Abilities		
101	Entitlement for nice things		
102	Lack of or not Powerful Aura/Energy field		
103	Body Attitude		
104	Outlook on Life		
105	Employment Stability		
106	Physical Strength		
107	Physical Health		
108	Fitness		
109	Sex (male or female)		
110	Race		
111	Reflexes		
112	Laugh		
113	Voice		
114	*Powerful Last Name		
115	*Hero/Celebrity/Fame Status		
116	Smell		
117	Vision		
118	Height		
119	Weight		
120	Body Shape		
121	Smooth Skin Face		
122	Smooth Skin Back		

123	Smooth Skin Chest		
124	Smooth Skin Arms		
125	Smooth Skin Legs		
126	Hair		
127	Eye Color		
128	Eye Shape		
129	Eyebrows		
130	Eyelashes		
131	Eyelids		
132	Eye Socket (bags etc).		
133	Nose		
134	Nostril		
135	Ears		
136	Ear Lobes		
137	Upper Lip		
138	Lower Lip		
139	Face		
140	Lack of Wrinkles		
141	Cheekbones		
142	Chin		
143	Head		
144	Forehead		
145	Arms		
146	Elbows		
147	Forearms		
148	Hands		
149	Palms		
150	Fingers		
151	Fingernails		
152	Knuckles		
153	Shoulders		
154	Cleavage		
155	Chest		
156	Breasts		
157	Nipples		
158	Stomach		
159	Lack of or not, Body Hair (upper body)		
160	Lack of or not, Body Hair (lower body)		
161	Lack of or not, Body Hair (back)		
162	Lack of or not, Facial Hair		
163	Upper Back		
164	Lower Back		
165	Body Type		
166	Accent		
167	Waist		
168	Hips		
169	Skin Tone		
170	Belly Button		
171	Love Handles		
172	Inner Thigh		
173	Outer Thigh		
174	Legs		
175	Knees		
176	Shins		
177	Feet		
178	Sole Feet		
179	Toes		
180	Toenails		

181	Lack of or not visible veins		
182	Neck		
183	Décolleté		
184	Calves		
185	Ankles		
186	Tongue		
187	Genitalia Shape		
188	Genitalia Size		
189	Genitalia Functionality		
190	Genitalia Pride		
191	Seductiveness		
192	Sexual Abilities		
193	Teeth		
194	Gums		
195	Smile		
196	Adam's Apple		
197	Wrists		
198	Flexibility		
199	Masculine		
200	Feminine		
201	Buttocks		
202	Dimples		
203	Lack of or not beauty marks		
204	Walk		
205	Stance		
206	Posture		
207	Presence		
208	Lack of or not Blemishes		
209	Tattoos/Body Art		
210	Body Piercing		
	TOTAL SCORE IS HOW ENTITLED YOU FEEL YOU ARE		TOTAL SCORE HERE

Note: Your Attention is your currency of "human energy."

The "multi-categorical" score-sheet gets more detailed later on

Doorway Five of reality

Teaching: The Five Energy Tiers

Energy Forms are infinite in the Universe, but finite here on earth (here are some I thought of)

It is impossible to measure the exact quality and quantity combination of each form of energy. The best way to look at these energy forms is through a crude sort of analysis. This is why I have broken them down into five tiers.

Tier Five

Absence of pain, acceptance, accomplishment, achievement, activity, action, admiration, adrenaline, advertisements, air, all living and non living things, all animals, all organisms, *all visible and invisible categories that make up a human being (see multicategorical score-sheet above), all religions, all spiritual thought, all thought of any kind, anniversary(s), appointments, anticipation, anything that can power anything to do work of any kind, anything new, a new journal, anything that feels "good" to you, anything worth money, anything from the "heart," appreciation, architecture, arousal, art, association (fraternity/sorority), associations (power of), auras, authority, awareness, balance, beach, beauty, being counted on, being interested, beliefs, belief system, birthday, bombs, breath, buildings, calendar date (see timing), caring, changes, coal, coincidences, concerts, comedy, compassion, compliment, concentration, conclusion, confidence, connection, consistency, contemplation, control, creating, credential, crowds anywhere, danger, deadlines, diesel, effervescence, electricity, entertainment (lose track of time), escape, event, excitement, exercise, expertise, eye contact, faith, family, favor, fear, feeling interested, feeling important, feeling organized, feeling loved, feeling needed, feeling rushed, feeling special, festivals, first impressions, forgiveness, food, foreplay, fuel, games, gasoline, gasoline, God, good fortune, graduation, gratefulness, gratitude, giving anything, heat, helping others, holidays (Halloween, Thanksgiving etc.), hope, "house money," improving in something, improving physical appearance, inspiration, intimacy, joy, knowledge, large crowds, laughter, learning, law suits, light, lightning, location, looking forward to seeing someone or doing something (opposite of dread), loyalty, love, loving someone or something, luck, lunar events, lust, manners, massage, meaning, memories, milestone, momentum, moon, music, nature, natural gas, new year's eve, new year's day, noise, nuclear energy, ocean, opportunity, organisms, organization, orgasms, paintings, points/goals/runs in a game, people pointing at something, people staring, personal collections, personal, pets, philosophy, personal values, physical space (taking up space), physical space (where you are), pictures, pills, playing a game, power, politeness, power, prayer, preparedness, pressure, pride, privacy, promotion at work, psychiatry, psychiatric pills, psychiatric diagnoses, purpose, receiving help, relaxing, relief, religion, reminders, responsibility, right of passage, ritual, romantic love, safety, security, seeing doctor, seeing lawyer, setting a record, sex, sentimental items, slogans, somebody listening to you, somebody unexpectedly pays for you, something that is expected to "cure" you, solar energy (all forms of "green energy"), sound, solutions, special access and/or privilege, special knowledge, special dates, space, stars, smile, stress, sun, suggestions (especially from parent or loved one), talking, thinking, the law, tone of voice, touching (physical), touching (emotional), trust, unexpected bonus,

ENLIGHTENMENT THROUGH ENTITLEMENT | 45

understanding, upward mobility, visible special badge or medal, variety, vibes, work, written words, wind, wisdom, water, zodiac sign. *Most of our energy comes from other people and/or the ambiance (atmosphere)*

The Crowd Matters Because The Crowd Creates The Ambiance

Ambiance is the mood, the vibe, and the atmosphere of a particular physical surrounding

We feed off of other people basically, and in order to make sense out of how much energy another has we subconsciously and/or consciously are forced to judge them. The specific ways in which we judge people are discussed in detail in the following doorways. For now let's be sure to understand that there is an inherent hierarchical structure to people with regards to quantity and quality of the energy that they emanate (physical appearance, family heritage/genetics etc.). In other words there are in fact "bad," "ok," and "good" families all the way up to royal families *in reality (and everything in between)*. The Walton's (Wal-Mart family), Dupont's, Rockefeller's, Bush's and Kennedy's of the world for example would be considered "good" families. Powerful families do in fact exist *in reality* and if you are born into one, you inherently (by your birthright and famous last name) have more energy (in this category only) than say a baby born into peasant class family from the middle of nowhere. The hierarchical structure is an always changing spinning karmic wheel dynamic of things and attributes a human being has or emanates to have. In many cases power and influence is quite fleeting actually and in other cases it can last for several generations. There are peasants—Kings/Queens based on genetics and famous last names and as stated every nuance in between. The genetics/lineage type categories are only part of what makes up the entire human being, but they are extremely important categories as it relates to feelings of *entitlement* (what this book is about). *This book is about the word entitlement and bringing awareness to what it means to feel "entitled." Entitlement is the force/energy in the Universe that is secretly controlling everything. Entitlement* is normal and natural in human beings and so is the inherent hierarchy the word implies. The world is in fact structured in a hierarchical way and this is part of *reality*. The periodic table of elements in Chemistry shows that certain elements by their very intrinsic nature have more or less atomic mass than other elements. There is a ranking to everything and become aware of this scientific truth. Beliefs and opinions can only take you so far. Eventually, every now and then, you'll bump up against truth. The truth I am referring to is that some people feel superior to other people and that is that. *Entitled* people should not have to feel bad or ashamed anymore about feeling *entitled* to nice things in life. Nepotism (perceived unfair favoritism of kin) is in the eyes of the beholder and is part of the natural order of the Universe. A family member usually will trust another family member more than a stranger. Why is this corruption? In the cutthroat nature of life, it is only natural and logical for each person to exploit every possible "advantage" they seemingly have. The *nature of reality* commands us to do so. Everyone must realize they too are equally selfish to feel good in life and in this regard we are all the same. The force of nature I am speaking about, if it could talk would say this "if you have an advantage; use it, if it opens doors, open them!" The problem inevitably arises when the "favored" family member begins to worry about the esteem and respect of his or her colleagues because it is looked down upon when someone was given something based on "family tradition." This is the double-edged sword *nature of reality*, as the person who was given the position based on family connections must deal with all kinds of guilty feelings associated with *entitlement* and so-called "advantages." As you will learn latter, these advantages mean nothing if peace of mind energy is not attained. The part of society that so-called "earned their own way" is probably a lot closer to peace of mind energy than the ones with the so-called "advantages." So who has a better life— the ones who follow a nepotistic model or the ones who make it own their own? The answer lies in who has more peace of mind energy and that is that and now clears the air for who has "more in life." The one who has "more" is the one who appreciates life more and can actually enjoy it. What good is nepotism if the so-called "beneficiary" is miserable all the time? Society in a way makes this person feel miserably guilty for what he or she has, doesn't understand him or her, and then (to make matters even worse) stigmatizes the whole thing as corruption of one kind or another, and simply can't comprehend how someone who seemingly has advantages can't appreciate things in life. The so-called "beneficiary" of the nepotistic model of *reality* is then in danger of severe misery as he or she is supposed to be able to "enjoy life" because he or she has "more" and a "better" position in life. The thing that keeps getting missed in this whole psychobabble non-sense is the **truth of energy exchanges between human beings.** People need people and feed off them for their energy needs. Each person desires an equilibrium exchange to feel most comfortable. If the so-called "beneficiary" of nepotism (many generations deep now say) is considered "higher up" in society, then by the hierarchical nature of reality invested in him or her, the higher up one goes, the less people he or she has to exchange equally with. In other words and in simple terms, the higher one goes up, the more rarified and confined one's social circle becomes. This is a crime in itself, but then to add on top of it, the complete misunderstanding that this "high" person should be happy with all his or her "advantages" only adds to the so-called "lucky" person's misery. He or she then begins to feel guilty that he or she has more, yet feels no appreciation for what he or she has. This is because most of our energy comes from other people and not inanimate objects. Inanimate objects cannot cure loneliness and cannot give one a sense of connection and integration with society that a human being so desperately needs. If one cannot find people to hang out with, and/or consistently feels drained after an evening out because the people weren't of his or her vibration or frequency—the ***root cause of depression*** is now found at last. It is the hierarchical structure of *reality* to blame and that is a truth and not a disorder of any kind. This condition happens at every level in society and it's all relative to who is exchanging with whom **socially.**

The Voice of a Generation

As you are now beginning to understand, it's all about **equilibrium with regards to human energy;** leaking, losing, or surging it (human energy) is **very painful** and this is a truth imbedded in **reality.** It's no fun being an outcast either on the low side or the high side because either way you are in a **VERY PAINFUL** human energy imbalance. Why should someone have to leak, implode, surge or lose energy to a society that doesn't understand or admit publicly to what actually goes on in **reality**? It's about time someone wrote a damn book about it!

"You can't say that to me, don't you know who I am? I'm so and so's son/daughter etc." is a mindset we must admit to in **reality.** I'm not making a moral judgment on such a mindset because **ultimately** the Universe doesn't care or judge. Like I said before, true and false exist, but right and wrong do not (with regards to morality). I am just stating the axiom that feelings of **entitlement** (entitlement energy) is secretly controlling all of mankind and is the **root cause** of all stress and conflict in our species. **PEOPLE FEEL** *ENTITLED* **TO HUMAN ENERGY EQUILIBRIUM.** It doesn't matter **WHERE** you fit in on the hierarchy of life as long as you can learn to play your level **EQUALLY AND FAIRLY.**

All other spiritual teachers need to get a clue of what **reality** is all about. Do not deny the powerful force of **entitlement.** If you deny it, you are blind to **reality.** *Awareness* (otherwise known as **enlightenment**) is in fact your best defense to **reality** (understanding every word of this book for example). Denial of **reality** is a "run, but you can't hide" dynamic. In other words and in plain English means this—*it will catch up to you* eventually so you might as well read it in print right now. It's just a **matter of time** until your **reality** blinders are forced off. Obviously some people will read this book at earlier ages than others. In general though, this generation (Generation X and all that are younger), is catching up faster than the generations before us because of such technological advances as the cell phone, e-mail, and the Internet. The human species was meant to evolve and consciousness of *reality* is part of this evolutionary process as we now move into higher energy states of *awareness* (the creation of this book for example). The age of *reality enlightenment* has now begun by virtue of this book being written. An honest and open debate about *reality* will uncover the truth to what we are in fact experiencing here on planet earth. *Reality* will go on trial in these writings and my expert witnesses will amaze you.

Tier Four

Since there are so many different forms of energy in the Universe (infinite), it would make sense to try and order them and make some sense of them. The human species quite simply is hard-wired to rank things so that we can make better sense of them. This is our survival instinct or our "will" at work. As you will soon find out, "will" exists, but it just isn't "free." This list here *is my opinion* of the four remaining tiers that energy forms should be categorized in. This is of course an inexact science and there is no way to calculate how much energy is being transferred around between human beings. This is why I have made a crude ordering system based on tiers and the order is *ultimately* up to you. This part of *the theory of reality* is an art not a science. I am just giving you some ideas of how the invisible energy Universe works in human behavior. There is plenty of actual real science later on in the teachings so don't worry about this theory not having a scientific backbone.

Passion, Meaningful Sex, Romantic Love or Infatuation Energy
= this energy makes you really interested in what you are doing. Time flies when you have this energy. It is a short-lived energy by its very nature, but extremely powerful when it happens.

Curiosity, Adventure, Exploration Energy = this energy allows you to keep moving into areas of life you have not experienced before. You either have a hunch you might like, or someone told you that you might like it. It's basically playing a hunch or intuition.

Awe, Magic, Wonder Energy = How'd that happen? Wow! I've got to learn more. "That was amazing, incredible and unbelievable." Think the 1980 US Olympic Men's Gold Medal Hockey Team and you got the energy this form represents.

Challenge Energy = they may not be fun, but this is the energy that forces you to "rise to the occasion" or perish. Something is in your way and you must conquer and if necessary destroy it.

Intimacy Energy = the feeling that one is not alone in this Universe, and can share all he or she wants with another while being true to oneself.

Friendship or Connection Energy = a lower form of intimacy energy. A type of sharing that makes one not feel completely alone in the Universe (just a little alone). This level of sharing is guarded, as friends do not share all their intimate secrets with one another.

Alive/Anger Energy = this energy is the energy of will. Not "free" will, just will. This energy is the opposite of suicidal ideation when externalized. This person simply wants to live and fight for no reason in particular other than to be alive. The opposite of this energy is that this person wants to die for no particular reason other than too tired to fight the war of life any longer.

Part of a Group Energy = the feeling or energy of taking a class, being on a sports team, just belonging somewhere at a certain time. This doesn't mean anything social, this just means being part of something other or bigger than oneself.

Acceptance of Circumstance, Appreciation of what one has,

Forgiveness Energy = basically you have what you have at this moment and that's that. Appreciate your life or you will resent it. Forgive everything in the past and live in the moment and plan for the future with an "I will never blame anyone or anything ever again" attitude for my problems.

Validation Energy = this is the energy or feeling we get when another person understands what you are feelings and says: "yes I have that feeling too."

Tier Three

Agitation/Stress/Ambivalence/Nervous Energy = it all starts here. If a person feels no discomfort, he is motivated to do nothing. Anxiety, stress, nervousness, whatever you want to call it, is the energy that powers us to do what we must do to relieve, reduce, eliminate, or avoid all forms of suffering each day we are alive. If you cannot find a way to relieve your suffering in a reasonable time to you, suicidal thoughts will inevitably come in because your body is looking for a solution. I wrote this book to relieve agitation energy and you were motivated to begin reading it for the same exact reason.

Winning/Victory Energy = one must be winning something of value to him or her and feel entitled to the winning. If one wins or is currently "winning" something and is cheating, lying, or not playing fairly, then this person will feel guilty. If you are a cheat or a fraud your body will let you know. You will feel the very deadly guilty energy associated with feelings of unworthiness. He or she will not feel the appreciation that comes with the win otherwise known as victory energy. Winning energy or victory energy is what is attained after the struggle has been won or one believes to be currently "winning." I am not talking about anything in particular; rather I am talking about the feeling of "winning" in the game/war of life. Victory or winning energy can only be attained if one feels entitled to the win or the "winning." One can in fact feel entitled to cheating and stealing etc. and therefore still attain victory or winning energy. Winning or victory energy is in the eyes of the beholder.

Tier Two

The "Big TEN" (in no particular order after #1)

1. ***Meaningful Task To Do Energy** = Having some task you "must do" or you won't feel right not doing it. In the Macro sense, it's Your Calling and You Must Do It. In the Micro sense, please see example at end of this tier.

People Energy = Other People who take up physical space, you pay attention to and pay attention to you.

Your Physical Environment/Space/Atmosphere (ambiance) Energy = What's in your visible and invisible space/surroundings (mostly comes from other People).

Timing Energy = "Timing is everything"—a powerful force which determines when things happen. Not why or how, just when. The dates on the calendar have a powerful force of energy all their own and is unique to each person. Examples: Wedding Date, Move Into New Home Date, and Start New Job Date etc. "If I can just make it to this date I'll be fine"

Internal Perceptions Energy = What you think of things and/or other people internally. Your thoughts attract the external world to you.

Physical Work/Labor Energy = This is your body in motion. It takes energy to do physical work whether or not you are paying attention to it is irrelevant.

Attention Energy = This is your currency for energy (not money energy). You use this currency to get all other forms of energy. Where your attention goes, your energy goes. Your attention span is your investment in yourself and you must use it wisely or be drained and lose out to others. The most comfortable feeling between humans is an equal exchange because any imbalance of human energy causes suffering. Getting too much or more than one feels entitled to causes guilt and a selfish need to give back energy. Getting to little causes resentment and depression and the selfish need to find more energy to even up the score.

Talking Energy When News Is Involved = This is the energy of conversation. "Sticks and stones may break my bones, but words can never hurt me" is the biggest bullshit line ever invented. Words are very powerful and when combined with tone can be deadly energy bullets. It all depends on who is saying what to you, when, and how much you respect their opinion. Talk is not cheap (especially at a psychiatrist's office). Regular "chit chat" or talking isn't that powerful however; in fact it's rather harmless. When there is "good" or "bad" news to be said—the energy of talking can make someone feel good or bad instantly depending on what the news means to their overall sense of well-being. News that involves an unexpected sudden change of plans and therefore alters one's sense of hope is a much more energized form of talking than news that pertains to a gradual change and/or is expected. This is because the nervous system (all human systems) needs to be re-conditioned slowly for optimal comfort.

Vortex Energy = This energy form was discussed in the preface. This energy is the whole reason why you are reading this book right now. This energy represents the visible manifestation point of the invisible collision point of the subconscious, conscious, opportunity, preparation, and timing. There are no coincidences or accidents in life. I know it is a cliché, but everything does happen for a reason (many reasons actually), it's just that you are not privy to all of them. Just because you do not know all the reasons why something has occurred does not mean they do not exist.

Fear of Death, A Big Loss, or Severe Illness = *This energy powers you to do things when you are afraid of your safety. You may all of a sudden need to buy something before a big hunting trip (say a knife) and because of this need; you will suddenly find the money and time to buy this crucial item. This is the energy that causes you to check and maintain things in proper order (say your car).*

* Example of why ***Meaningful Task To Do Energy is number one in Tier 2.***

Pretend there was a royal family in New York and one of its members loved ice hockey and the New York Rangers. Say he wanted to be a "true fan" and get all the best tickets for all the best games but because he was such a rabid fan wanted to be "with the people" otherwise known as the "regular fan." Each year he knew the tickets for the season went on sale at 9am on a certain day, but in order to get good seats he would have to wait on line starting the night before. He had heard people started to line up at 5pm-7pm the night before and camped out on the pavement outside of Madison Square Garden.

Now this extremely wealthy individual (from a royal family don't forget) could've easily gotten the tickets through ticket-master, a ticket broker, or more likely would already have season tickets, but would not find that as "meaningful" as staying up all night on the dirty sidewalk like all the "real fans."

Question: What is the point of this example?
Answer: The point is this. The trump card for people energy, environment energy, and all the energies listed in Tier 2 can be trumped (over-ruled, superceded) by having

a "meaningful task to do." Once you have ***Meaningful Task To Do Energy (short-lived energy or long-term version of it and everything in between)***, you won't care who the people are around you or what the physical environment is like. All you want to do is your "meaningful task" at hand and nothing will bother you because you are there for a reason and can answer the all-important why to as why you are doing a particular task. Once ***Meaningful Task To Do Energy* is depleted enough**, runs down to a flicker, or is completed then all the other energy forms will matter once again. To be clear, ***Meaningful Task To Do Energy (you can consider this your "work")*** is the trump card for all other energies of Tier Two and can prove to be a lifesaver when you don't like the people you are around or the physical environment you find yourself in. Find a "meaningful task to do" and you'll block out the energy leak of the other energies around you which are causing you discomfort. If you cannot find ***Meaningful Task To Do Energy*** then the people, environment, timing, and all the other energies matter and will affect the way you feel.

Before we get to the "medal round" I would like to covert "human energy" to real "energy" so that you the reader can better visualize what exactly it is this discussion is all about. In tier five, the energy form of "exercise" is mentioned. Recently in the Northeast we had a record blackout that caused the power to go out for about fifty million people. Let me take you to an imaginary theoretical city (say New York in the year 2100) where all the health clubs are considered by law "back up" generators in case of such a crisis occurring. In such a power outage emergency, the law states that "all able bodied citizens" would be asked to "work out" and donate "their energy." People in the past have been asked to donate blood of course, but never energy. Anyway—as the citizens of the great thriving metropolis began to run on the treadmills, stationary bikes, elliptical trainers, and rowing machines etc, all this energy would be hooked up to the power grid and literally create energy for our own human use. You see, people do in fact have energy and it could (in theory) be converted to "real" energy. The same dynamic is at work with regards to all the forces of nature (wind, water, solar etc.). The windmills (think Holland) of the world do in fact convert energy from nature (wind) for human purposes. Humans in theory are able to do the same exact thing—if our running, rowing, and stair-mastering were simply converted onto the power grid. Our emotions are the invisible part of the energy world as they too are human energy, but there is no way to calculate how much energy they contain. However—if you are very angry, you may run for many more hours on the treadmill as you let your emotion (anger) power you as you convert it onto the treadmill. If you feel weak, you won't be able to run that much because you are "zapped" of life, "zapped" of energy. The Laws of Physics are coming in a few doorways and that is where all the science behind the ***theory of reality*** is proven.

Question: What is the whole point of what I am saying?
Answer: The point of this book is to prove to you the reader and the world (one reader at a time) that the ***root cause of mental illness*** is not faulty brain chemistry or a chemical imbalance in the brain, but rather the transfer of energy amongst people. A theory by its very definition is not scientifically provable (that's why it's a theory/hypothesis) and we must always remember that with all the competing theories surrounding mental illnesses (this one now added to the list). But I maintain clearly, that my theory is in fact the one that has it correct and is true.

So I leave you with this: The current theory of psychiatry **is more outlandish and less provable than my theory.** I have simply created here another branch, another theory that should rival and be compared to the present improvable theory of *root causation of mental illnesses*. In short, it will now be "the brain chemistry theorists" versus "the human energy transfer theorists." I believe my theory will clearly separate itself as a superior theory as time and people evolve further into higher energy states of *awareness of reality*.

Quite Simply

The psychiatric profession will never be able to prove the *root causation* of mental illness is hiding in brain chemistry or chemical imbalances. The entire anti-depressant/mood stabilizer industry is in fact a forever-outlandish improvable scam. It is all placebo or anti-placebo depending on what your belief system is. If you take one of these pills and feel better because of the pills (so you believe) that's great for you (you gain energy via the belief that the pill does in fact work), but there is no proof that it is the pill making you feel better. Psychiatric pills are crutches that have no provable basis in math or science. I believe it is the powerful placebo energy that the pill represents that is making you feel better. The pill represents the doctor who told you it would work, your friends and relatives who said the pills work, the feeling you are not alone because these pills exist due to people like you, and the expectation that they will work. The more you look up to, respect, and worship the doctor who prescribed them to you, the more likely the pills will work for you and that is that. I'm just stating that anti-depressants, anti-psychotics (which help with thinking in theory—like they could figure out a pill that makes one think "clearer" etc.) These pills are not, and never will be scientifically provable #1 and #2 who made doctors the authorities on how to think? Who died and made these people messiahs? Nobody can say or has the authority to say what is "clear thinking" and what is not. I am only refuting pills in this world that claim they work on a person's chemical imbalance in the brain or a person's "brain chemistry." There are many pills on planet earth *that are scientifically provable*, but these classes/types of pills *are not* some of them.

A word about the energy forms in tiers 5-2. Energy ranking is a tricky business and what I have attempted to do is simply crudely rank them. The rankings are in my perception and your perception of how they rank may be different. That's fine. The point is that everything in life is ranked and that there are different energy forms at work in our daily lives. Welcome now to tier number One (in my perception).

Doorway Six of reality

Teaching: The Medal Round

Tier One
BRONZE Medal of life

Control of Equilibrium Energy on demand = this is the most superior form of *victory or winning energy*. This includes the *BIG TEN from Tier #2*. The BIG TEN are the ten energy forms we seek to control the most often because they are so much more valuable than the other energies (this is why they are in tier # two). These ten once again are meaningful task to do, people, atmosphere, timing, internal perceptions, attention, physical work/labor, fear of death, loss or severe injury, talking and vortex energy.

    Once we no longer have a MEANINGFUL TASK TO DO will OTHER PEOPLE matter again. Herein lies the trick of life: People help create and are the backbone of the atmosphere (the crowd) that we see, so people by their very presence are a **DOUBLE WHAMMY**. People are people and people are part of the atmosphere (ambiance). You have to now become aware to what the whole fight in our species is all about—**CONTROLLING HUMAN ENERGY** so that you and not someone else will get their entitled share (there isn't enough to go around to satisfy each person's unique entitlement issues).

Once again small review time:

The People/Atmosphere Trump Card

***HAVING A MEANINGFUL TASK TO DO ENERGY**—with this energy, you will not care who the people are or what the atmosphere (physical environment) is like that you are in. You will just want to do your task and get out and on with your life. This is the #1 form of energy from TIER TWO because it can TRUMP and OVER-RIDE the people and atmosphere of any given situation.*

As soon as you understand what is going on *in reality* will the contest begin for you. The fight is about this: What is the most *control of equilibrium energy on demand* that you are allowed by society and/or the Universe to have? How much do you feel *entitled* to? *Entitlement* is hiding here because well for starters *entitlement* is hiding everywhere all the time behind everything visible and seemingly "obvious." Everyone has a different amount of energy they *need* in order to attain *control of equilibrium energy on demand.* Notice the word *need* and not want. The word *need* implies *entitlement* because it is in reality a *need.* Without the energy one *needs* to survive—"mental illness" will set in and self-destruction or suicidal ideation will rule the human being. The "mental illness" *is an energy defense mechanism to force attention* or other forms of human energy onto the human being (money energy, attention, other various resources such as "take care of me or I'll die" etc.). The battle for scarce finite human energy has now begun. Make no mistake about it; *entitlement energy* is secretly behind everything, behind every so-called "mental illness" and life is a full-blown competition/war for human energy (the amount we feel we deserve/entitled to). Families fight over money energy, people fight for attention and love. You cannot deny the fierce brutal nature of reality here on earth—for human energy.

Question: What exactly is *"control of equilibrium energy on demand?"*
Answer: *Control of equilibrium energy on demand* is the ability to avoid, relieve, reduce, or eliminate all forms of suffering whenever one desires. *Th is is the form of energy that people fight for every second of every day.*
Question: May I have a simplified example of *controlling equilibrium energy on demand?*
Answer: A good example of *controlling equilibrium energy on demand* would be the "day at the beach example." Pretend you are at your favorite beach in the middle of July and the sun is blazing down on you. The sun's energy is extremely strong on this particular day and you are *aware of* its potential harm to your skin if adjustments to its energy are not made. Each person has his or her own *equilibrium point* with regards to controlling the sun's energy. Some people stay under a beach umbrella, others stay in the ocean, and others lie in the sun *with different degrees and amounts* of sun tan lotion/block applied to their bodies. Another way to control the sun's energy is to simply control the amount of time outdoors in it or around it at this particular moment on this particular day. At any time you are free to stop paying attention to it (stop exchanging with it), and go indoors and do something else. The point is this: the only comfortable zone with regards to feeling well when it comes to energy defense and protection is equilibrium and the perceived control of it. Each person has different wants, **needs**, and desires (getting a nice tan for example) when it comes to how much energy they are comfortable with (once again, **entitlement** is hiding here). Applying lotion comes in various degrees of strength (SPF # on the bottle) and how often and liberally the lotion is applied also matters. Each person has his or her unique point of equilibrium with regards to controlling

the sun's energy as it powers towards us. The whole trick is to not take too much or you'll get burnt, but not take too little either or else you'll get too cold. Take just the amount you feel you deserve *(need)*.

Question: Another example?
Answer: *Being able to go to the bathroom whenever one desires. Going to the bathroom feels good because we go back to human energy equilibrium (with regards to human waste) and get rid of excess energy that we are carrying around. Our body alerts us to the discomfort of carrying around too much energy and seeks to find equilibrium. If it could talk it would say, "we need to go to the bathroom to be more comfortable as we seek energy equilibrium."*

Suffering

Question: What kind(s) of suffering are we talking about?
Answer: All the forms that you perceive exist. The list includes agitation, stress, anxiety, mental, intellectual, spiritual, psychic, meta-physical, psychological, physiological, physical, emotional, existential etc. **ALL CONCEIVABLE FORMS OF HUMAN SUFFERING.**

The mystery behind suffering has nothing to do with a "chemical imbalance" in the brain, faulty "brain chemistry," or such things as chronic fatigue syndrome cause by a virus nobody can fully explain properly or definitively as the psychiatric/medical professions and drug companies will have you believe. Many people have the Epstein-Barr virus or have had it yet do not or did not have chronic fatigue syndrome—Why? Keep reading. Suffering is an energy imbalance and the theories brought forward in these teachings are in fact **more provable** and **less outlandish** than the current theories used by the psychiatric and medical professions today. Neither psychiatrist nor doctor nor **Drug Company Inc.** will teach **reality** because they either don't know it, or are not financially motivated to do so.

Human Energy Imbalance Degrees

The too little energy side = missing, cutting, losing, puncturing, dripping, leaking, bleeding, or hemorrhaging invisible energy. The too much energy side = pressurizing, gaining, surging, infusing, clotting, bursting, imploding, or having an aneurysm of invisible energy.

If you have too much or too little energy, you will feel the suffering that begs for you to be in energy balance (equilibrium) once again. Your body will try and force the equilibrium issue for you. If you have too little you will walk slowly, move slowly, and act depressed. If you have too much, you will act hyper, want to exercise, feel "manic," and want to take on the world. In other words, it is the energy deficit or surplus causing all emotions and moods *not* brain chemistry, chemical imbalances in the brain, or viruses (Epstein-Barr etc.).

Now the whole point of life

Basically any psych patient will feel better when they feel there is *"enough"* in it for him or her (situation specific or overall life). Not just something "in it" for him or her, but *ENOUGH*. Once again our old friend *entitlement* is hiding out again and is hiding deep in the word *"ENOUGH."*

Everything everyone/anyone does or says is deeply rooted in cost-benefit analysis (of human energy).

Whether or not it is conscious or subconscious is not relevant at this stage of the teachings. Just be sure to understand that *entitlement* causes the dynamic of *cost-benefit analysis of *LIFE* (whether it's even worth living or not) to be different for each person based on *entitlement* issues that *are based on the overall score of the "multi-categorical" score-chart/score-sheet.*

* *Cost-benefit analysis usually means money energy and rightfully so. The answer to whether something is "worth it" is hiding in your feelings and your body*

People feel better as they connect with **enough** energy in their external worlds. As discussed earlier, people get most of their energy from other people and the ambiance they are in. You need to simply find the people, person or situation that re-awakes you and has **"enough"** in "it" for you. "It" is life. A "manic" person is a person with too much energy and needs to balance it (up all night working, exercise addict etc.). A so-called "depressed" person is someone with too little energy (can't get out of bed, walks very slowly) and is also trying to balance it (forcing attention or money on him or her for example). It's all about the energy balancing machines that we human beings are. Labeled "depression" or mania (manic-depression/bi-polar) is simply an energy imbalance and this is the discovery of these writings.

Question: It seems as if *too much energy* or *too little energy* is harmful. What then is one to do?
Answer: An easy answer for this stage of the teachings is this: Simply listen to your body very carefully and go where you need to go to meet the person or people you need to meet **at the time** (jail, psych ward, whatever). **THE ONLY JOB YOU HAVE ON THIS PLANET IS TO LISTEN TO YOUR BODY AND READ THE MESSAGES IT GIVES YOU. IT'S ALL "IN THERE."**

Happy Traveling on your ultimately neutral assignment of evolution on planet earth!
As you read these teachings you will understand why this is true later on. You will begin to understand **reality**. There are many doorways to go through and the teaching on "free will"

being an illusion is vital. The **golden key to reality** will open up doorway number seven.

Question: Why is *control of equilibrium energy on demand* the constant fight in mankind?
Answer: This is where **entitlement** is lurking. There is not enough *control of equilibrium energy on demand* to go around to satisfy each person's unique **entitlement** issues. Everyone cannot be a King or a Queen though everyone tries to be *initially* (in their own way). As stated previously, **entitlement** issues are secretly controlling everything (all human behavior).
Question: What's more likely to cause suffering—having too little energy or too much energy?
Answer: Too little energy (energy leakage) is more common because having too much energy is kind of hard to do actually (having *too much* money for example). Everyone radiates a certain amount of energy and the whole trick is to feel **entitled** to it. It is not that difficult to feel **entitled** to a lot since the world is inherently dangerous and a stockpile of energy seems like a pretty good idea. "Rainy days" do happen and we are aware of this fact. In preparation of hard times, having an abundance of energy is in fact a good defense against life. If one does feel "over-abundance" with regards to energy, this means he or she simply doesn't feel *entitled* to it. This is where the emotion of guilt is hiding. If you do have perceived undeserving energy and feel this imbalance—you have three options. Option #1 is that you can give it away and delude yourself that you are being selfless (teach something, do charity/volunteer work, or give it away). Option #2 is the same as number one only now you are aware (you read this book say) and understand

that true altruism doesn't exist. You are only giving your energy away so that you can selfishly erase the guilt you feel. You are aware that as you slowly unload your energy, your goal is to only be left with exactly what you feel you deserve. Option #3 is that you can simply feel ***entitled*** to it. This will cure the guilt you feel for having "too much."

Question: Can you simplify this?

Answer: Yes. Just make sure you understand all the different degrees and nuances. For the remainder of this text we will stick with losing or gaining energy (to keep things simpler).

Question: What do you mean by such terms as losing or gaining energy?"

Answer: Once again and to be crystal clear, suffering is caused by *too little energy or too much energy.* Contrary to what many people may think, humans only desire what they feel ***entitled to.*** *The problems inevitably arise when two or more people feel* ***entitled*** *to the same exact thing.* This is inevitable since internal perceptions are infinite. This means everyone tries to be a King or Queen of sorts until checked and balanced by another. If we receive less than what we feel ***entitled*** *to*, we get pissed off and resentful. "This is not the life I signed up for, I deserve better than this, and this isn't fair or right." Sound familiar? If we receive more energy than we feel ***entitled*** to, we feel guilty. As stated, *control of equilibrium energy on demand* is the constant fight we are in, and each living creature has different **entitlement** issues for where their unique state of equilibrium is.

A perceived equal exchange of energy is what we secretly desire. Credit for who we perceive we are. Energy in = energy out (All the Laws of Physics are on my side as you will understand later on)

Question: Can you lose energy at the same exact time as gain energy?

Answer: Every situation, thought, and moment is either a mixture of the two sides of the energy equation or all of one side. In theory, if you had the same amount of both in any given moment (same amount of loss with the same amount of gain), they would balance out (50/50) and you'd feel fine (in equilibrium). Every situation is different on a moment-to-moment basis. You can lose energy one second and then gain it the next. Once you understand that *controlling equilibrium energy on demand* is the energy form you need to start feeling better about yourself will you be able to grapple with the **SILVER MEDAL** energy form coming up next. In other words, in order to get *control of equilibrium energy on demand* takes a certain amount of **MONEY ENERGY** that only you know how much you *need*. It is different for everybody. Our old friend *entitlement* is once again hiding here in **MONEY ENERGY** because *entitlement energy* is hiding everywhere all the time remember? Let the real war begin now as we graduate now to the *SILVER MEDAL of life*

SILVER MEDAL of life

$MONEY$ Energy with regards to ENTITLMENT Energy for it

Entitlement Energy = one must feel *entitled* to something by virtue of being a citizen of planet earth and all the *agitation energy* that goes with it. It is our birthright to feel *entitled to energy* since this is what we are made of. We all feel *entitled* to energy, but the only question left is how much do we feel we "deserve." Energy (*agitation energy etc.*) is what powers us and makes us go, to be alive, to be human. We are made of energy concealed by our earth suits (skin). We secretly feel *entitled* to be as miserable or joyous as what we perceive the average person to be and we all need different amounts of money energy to attain human energy equilibrium. We secretly feel *entitled* to get what we feel we "deserve." We are *entitled* to our depressions if we can't figure out a way to get what we need because we force attention onto us and are in need of energy equilibrium. We measure ourselves multi-categorically against others and secretly rank who is "higher" or "lower." People do feel superior/equal/inferior to others and this is a fact of life. Getting what one feels ENTITLED to is in the eyes of the beholder as we all seek human energy equilibrium. To be simple and frank—we all have different amounts of money energy we need to feel "comfortable" on planet earth.

$MONEY$ Energy

Life is an expensive habit and in order to control the **BIG TEN in tier two** *takes money*. Money talks, bullshit walks. Money supply though sometimes increased by the Federal Reserve is obviously finite. Money Energy (and the *entitlement* feelings behind it to have it) is the 2nd most powerful form of *ultimately* impersonal, *ultimately* impartial, and *ultimately* neutral energy. The reason for this is quite simple. *Money energy* can control the **"BIG TEN" from tier two. For example, money can control and force** another person's attention on you (whether it is a massage therapist or a doctor you get the idea). In theory if you had unlimited, ungodly sums of money, you could live in the most beautiful, most expensive psychiatric hospital known to man (you would have built it and currently would run it). People would be hired just to make sure you felt fine as much as humanly possible. This does not mean you will be happy living there, I am just stating what you could do in theory. Every second of every day someone would be asking you "how do you feel?" and "do you need anything?" All is fun and games until someone gets the bill. This constant fight for **money energy** is very real and reeks with personal responsibility, emotional baggage, psychological defenses, existential undertones, intellectual reasoning, and **EVERYTHING AND ANYTHING** that makes up a human being. The subconscious, conscious, and all conditioned human energy reeks with money energy and everything you do is a money energy vortex. EVERYTHING IN LIFE is a COST-BENEFIT analysis and it is always and easily felt in one's own body. Was that worth it (the money energy)? Your physical body will tell you yes, no, maybe yes or maybe not. If it's a close call **ambivalence energy** seeps in from tier three which will force you to become clearer. Ambivalence/nervousness, agitation, stress whatever you want to call it will beg, insist and demand you find energy equilibrium once again. So if you overpaid (resentment) for something or underpaid (guilt) you will find equilibrium the next time or if not the next time so on and so forth. Your body will not rest until you get it right. **EVERYTHING** is hiding in **ENTITLEMENT** and **MONEY ENERGY** and how the two are related to one another on an individual level of people sizing each other up in the hierarchy of life, and the internal perceptions one has of oneself on the "multi-categorical" score-sheet. "Who is going to pay for this?" "Whose fault is it?" The answer is *ultimately* no one or *ultimately* everyone. Everyone is a "spoiled brat," it's just a question of degree.

Question: Where does it end?
Answer: Let's stop this nonsense and insanity right here, right now. While we are here living in *reality*, the buck has to always stop with someone (who will pay for what and why). The buck stops here now with *ultimately impersonal energy* (me) as the biggest monster of the subconscious is now brought into consciousness. Even more so than death, *money and entitlement* (and

how they are inter-related) is by far the most denied aspect of human existence. Everybody knows it deep down inside, yet no one wants to talk about this extremely dirty subject matter that reeks of and with **entitlement** issues. Well, guess what nobody on this planet will take less than they feel they deserve or more than they deserve without the emotional energy that is used in each transaction to make it a zero sum game. Your body will make it a zero sum game, as cost-benefit analysis (survival instinct) is hard-wired into your energy being. Now that I've got you on human energy terms, you can now understand why the **SILVER MEDAL** goes to **money with regards to entitlement issues energy**. Be aware it is the most **powerful ultimately impersonal** energy form and you are well on your way to reality awareness (otherwise known as **ENLIGHTENMENT**). We are all energy balancing machines and our conditioned human energy systems will make absolutely sure you get what you deserve in life.

Other spiritual teachers make a very big deal of what the word *"enlightenment"* means and talk for endless hours on what it means to be "enlightened." Well, I can explain it in one word— **AWARENESS**. The book's title is *Enlightenment through Entitlement* because once you become aware of the secret force controlling everything—*entitlement* (for money energy) can you become fully aware and awake to the true nature of reality. Only through this understanding, which is basically, an understanding of the "multi-categorical" score-sheet can you become aware of reality—otherwise known as *enlightenment*.

Do not listen to people who say their favorite defense "what do you expect, life isn't fair? Who said life is fair?"

Tell them to read this book and to understand the Physics part of energy systems coming up later. **Energy in = Energy out.** Always has and always will. You must understand the premise however—that human beings are energy balancing machines and *AIM TO MAKE IT FAIR*. Life will in fact be made fair and is fair (in the long run). *We are on this planet to make it fair.* We are forced by nature to try and even out the score. People always say the same stupid stuff to each other—"life isn't fair." This is bullshit because it is our duty as human beings to make it fair in our perceptions. "Fair" is in the eyes of the beholder, and we simply will not allow to be taken advantage of. This is exactly how our assignments get played out—the desire to make it a "perceived fair and equal exchange of our energy." Lawsuits, medical bills, friends, relatives, health, parents all have strings attached *rooted* in *money energy*. I am not ashamed to admit that I have been in a few psychiatric hospitals (genius or crazy you decide) due to stress in which everything was "no problem" and "don't worry your insurance will take care of it." Then later, *time after time,* the insurance company would refuse to pay the hospital for one reason or another (claiming missing paperwork or lack of authorization)—*in reality* some way of trying to worm out of it which would in turn force the hospital to come after me for the payment. So nobody really gives a shit about you *ultimately*, all they want is to do their jobs and *get paid*. They continually send bills to an already stressed out person routinely causing their distress to worsen. You call this a society that actually cares how people feel and a society based on kindness? Insurance companies due everything in their power to not cover mental health situations even if you are one hundred percent covered. *It is their job to find a way not to pay the huge hospital bills.* This is where *reality* is hiding—in the fight over who pays what and why because *money energy* is so hard to get, so *rooted* in *entitlement (who gets what and why),* and so deeply entrenched in the subconscious emotional underworld that nobody really wants to talk about it on the surface because it's so damn dangerous to do so. It's when the bills/invoices come quietly closing in on you, "slipped" into the mailbox, into the *impersonal* mail that *reality* reveals itself. Is reality ugly? Well I say it's neutral, but since we are so conditioned not to bring up such subjects, many people reading this will say my viewpoint is that reality is ugly. Why must it be "ugly" or "beautiful" and not "neutral?" It is what it is—a fierce brutal competition for equilibrium energy based on entitlement feelings.

Back to my example:

> Long after all the doctors seemed so nice and rosy to you when in you inter-faced with them. Insurance companies routinely fight hospitals and hospitals have no choice but to eventually bill the already vulnerable patient. At the time, everyone says the same silly things just to avoid a conflict—"don't worry about the payment—it'll be taken care of." I call bullshit on that and now back *to reality*.
> *Wake up world, this life is for fighting and for wars*
> *Yes—It is about money energy and the ultimately impersonal fight over it—make no mistake about this secret war.* EVERYTHING and I MEAN EVERYTHING *is a cost-benefit analysis. Each human being wants and demands what he or she feels entitled to and that is that.*
> *Energy in = Energy out*
> You think insurance companies want to pay your health claims like they said they would easily and without conflict? Each and every time they play a game with the cooperating hospital and try and delay the payment as long as humanly possible. They do eventually pay, but only after delay after delay which is part of how they do business. People need to **GET PAID. THERE IS NO FREE LUNCH AND NOTHING CLOSE TO "SELFLESSNESS" ON PLANET EARTH.** Yes there are so called "good people" but they are only "good people" when **THEY GET PAID** (in money or in some other human energy form). Anyone who says they are "volunteering to help people" is really saying, "I want to volunteer and help people because it makes me feel good about myself."

"Dr. Mr. So and So,

On August 1st we received a denial of payment for the services rendered to you by your insurance company xyz. We are now appealing this decision not to authorize payment for your Adult Inpatient Mental Health services concerning your stay here at XYZ Hospital. We will complete our review and render a determination in this matter by Aug 29th. In the meantime please feel free to call us at xxx-xxx-xxxx. Please refer to claim # xxxxxxxx if you have any questions.

Sincerely,
XYZ Hospital Treatment Coordinator

Not to mention:
From the New York Post in 2002

"FISCAL AGONY LINGERS LONG AFTER SURGICAL PAIN"

Lenox Hill Hospital helped repair a 22-year-old woman's broken neck. Now it may break her back—financially.

The Manhattanite fell and broke a neck vertebrae in April while finishing college in Pennsylvania. After being stabilized in a local hospital, she was transferred to Lenox Hill for surgery. "I had a 50/50 chance of walking again," she said. Her two surgeries were a success, but the patient—who asked not to be identified—nearly died when she got the bill.

The hospital is asking her to pay $83,699—the charges remaining after her $50,000 student insurance policy capped out.—

The biggest charge on the Lenox Hill bill is $52,800 for room and board—$4,400 a day for a 12-day stay—a rate she calls "incomprehensible."

Lenox Hill has since raised its rate for a semi-private room to $6,179.

While nursing care was included, she was also forced to hire a private nurse for one night after her first surgery to get the attention she needed—

Lenox Hill spokeswoman Ann Silverman did not respond to The Post's questions about the woman's bill. The woman also got no answers from hospital administrators.

Note: The $6,179 is the rate the hospital charges for its cheapest room per night, shared by two patients—complete with those ugly curtains between beds. A couple of ibuprofen costs an additional $4.

You can fool yourself into thinking the world is not a fierce jungle for energy and become blind to it. You can cheat yourself out of truth until your blind basically. Why not learn the truth and accept it as *reality* instead of running from it? It will catch up to you anyway that this life, this planet is for fighting and for wars. Period.

Now obviously mistakes happen, once in a while, but when one is confronted over and over again with the same exact superficial "game," the same exact "war," some truths become self-evident. Then when one asks several friends and family members if this same exact thing has happen to them and they all say yes, then we know a full blown "call to arms" about money energy is in order. Like I said, the buck stops here. Your subconscious will now awake to the second most valuable energy form in the Universe. Here the truth will show you that *entitlement* for this energy form is intrinsically powerful, as no one will surrender one more penny than they feel they have to. Make no mistake about it, very personal money energy, yet *ultimately* impersonal money energy is behind everything. Who takes responsibility for something is the person who pays the damn bill regardless if they verbally own up to it or not. We are a racist society. We do not favor black or white. We favor "green" as in *money energy*. This is the only race that truly matters. Money talks, bullshit walks. This should not come as a surprise to you. Now money does not buy happiness or "peace of mind." As you will read very soon, "peace of mind energy" reigns supreme in the Universe however it is very elusive and difficult to attain.

Therefore, this teaching simply states that if you cannot attain the **GOLD MEDAL** of life, and must settle for the **SILVER**, then it is much better to be a rich miserable person than a poor miserable person. Fight for every dime, and don't let anyone say to you "it's only money." If they say that to you—"relax, it's only money," then say, "great—if it's *only money* you pay for it." See how quickly they run for the hills. In other words let them pay your bills if it's such a silly thing to fret over. Watch how fast they change their tune on the "it's only money" song and dance. Its *only money* when it's not *your money*. It's easy to spend other people's money, but when it yours—well everything changes. Do not cave in, do not be passive, fight for your *entitled money energy* because if you don't someone else will take it and laugh themselves all the way to the bank on your behalf. You'll end up in a state hospital without any power in this constant fight and dependent on others. They will say you have a mental illness as a defense to you not being able to function. All you have is energy imbalance syndrome as you didn't even realize that there is an invisible war going on between people every second they (we) are together. In short, don't lose your pride. People make a living out of being "a good person" meanwhile they're robbing you blind. They say the are "here to help you." Yeah right—as long as they get paid (in some form of energy). There is no free lunch on planet earth and *money energy* secretly permeates clashing *entitlement for safety*. I freely and openly admit as the author of this book, that I desire energy in return—money energy for my effort in writing this book. This book is a product of Law #1 as is all human behavior. *Law #1* will be drilled into you as we go forward together.

Question: What form of energy is most likely to cause change?
Answer: Everything in life has the subconscious (human energy system conditioning) "cost-benefit" analysis (with regards to energy) going on in the invisible energy world. *Money Energy* is the number one way to create change in human behavior. Give someone

"ENOUGH" in it for him or her and watch him or her begin to work. Tell them their insurance will no longer pay and watch them leave the psychiatric hospital and suddenly get "better." If there is nothing on the outside (not ENOUGH in it for him or her) that the psych patient views as "worth it" they will prefer to live on the inside and go bankrupt (*money energy*). In a way they win because they no longer care. They have surrendered in the battle of life. The *motivational force of money energy is unrivaled.*

Money Energy with regards to entitlement issues, not death is the number one energy form hidden and denied in the subconscious. The reason for this is that money reeks with *entitlement* issues meaning who will do what for what price $$. **Money Energy** is the vortex where all *entitlement* issues are hiding.

Law #1—All human thought and action (including this book) has evolved to be one hundred percent defensive, protective, selfish, and self-serving so that one can avoid, relieve, reduce, or completely eliminate all forms of suffering via a perceived equal and fair exchange of energy. Overall human energy balance (equilibrium) is what we seek and deserve. Human energy imbalance is the *root cause* of all conceivable forms of human suffering and *all mental illnesses.*

Question: What is stress?
Answer: A human energy imbalance rooted in entitlement issues.

Next Stop THE GOLD—
THE GOLD MEDAL of life
Peace of Mind Energy

GOLD MEDAL of life

*Perceived "True Love" Energy or Perceived "Soulmate" Love Energy = the endgame = peace of mind energy

THIS IS WHERE WE HARMONIZE ALL ASPECTS OF BEING A HUMAN BEING. ALL FACTORS THAT MAKE US BE HUMAN FEEL IN BALANCE. WE ARE GETTING EXCATLY WHAT WE FEEL ENTITLED TO. THERE IS NO JEALOUSY, NO DESIRE FOR "MORE" and NO DESIRE TO HAVE LESS, NO GUILT FOR WHAT WE HAVE. THIS IS HOW WE HARMONIZE.

Peace of Mind Energy (aware or unaware) = This form of energy is a tricky concept and to understand *reality*, one must understand this energy form fully. People do not want to feel *too safe* or *too in control* of everything around them because then insufferable boredom sets in. To evolve to superior energy form #1 and attain the *gold medal of life* means this: *to feel in control of being slightly out of control and to still be in equilibrium.*

Awareness Energy = this is basically the energy you will have if and when you understand the theories and teachings of this book and accept them as truth. Warning: *awareness energy* is almost always *initially* very painful. Once you attain *awareness energy* you will be cloaked in the most powerful invisible force there is. *Awareness energy* is the best defense to life. To be aware is to accept the fifteen laws of human energy dynamics (see doorway nine). Wake up to the fact that *control of equilibrium energy on demand* is what we are all fighting for which takes your unique amount of **money energy** and then, only the, you will have earned the silver medal of life. You are now aware and awake to the brutal and fierce warlike nature of *reality*.

Peace Of Mind Energy

This means allowing such energies as curiosity, challenge, adventure, and a little risk in your life to come in, but not overwhelm you. You are in control of being slightly out of control. You need *money energy* to allow all of these things (just the amount you feel *entitled* to).

The trick is this: one must take risks in life to feel truly alive, but not too much risk or one will feel "out of control." The other tricky part is that each person has a different breaking point as to where the risk is too much for him or her to handle. The breaking point is the point where a person goes from being in control of slightly out of control energy to *out of control* of slightly out of control energy.

The whole trick of life is to find this tricky type of energy equilibrium on demand and *the amount of money energy* one needs (feels *entitled* to), and to be aware of what of what you are doing as you attempt to control all the variables around you (as much as humanly possible).

Once you have done all you can do, then *aware with peace of mind energy* will settle in. It's a moment-to-moment thing however.

Aware with peace of mind energy is the endgame for each person and is the goal of all human beings. It is extremely competitive to get this energy form and be aware of that. Also note that all paths are equal as long as the human being in question can find *peace of mind energy (aware or unaware).* *This means the intellectual reading this is equal to the unaware peasant. The unaware peasant is on a lower vibration yes, but they don't need much to feel peace of mind energy. The money energy part is insignificant to them. Wealthy "peaceful" people need more to be in equilibrium that's all.*

In *reality*, it doesn't matter how one gets this energy (peace of mind aware or not) since the Universe is *ultimately* impersonal, *ultimately* impartial, and *ultimately* neutral. All that matters is the *awareness* and conscious evolutionary process that this is what we are after. *Aware with peace of mind energy* is so extremely elusive and so fast changing that I wouldn't dare attempt to write an iron clad lesson on how to get it (this is the best I can offer you since I'm still trying to find it myself). This is edition one after all. All I know is that this energy form reigns supreme in the Universe. Have it and you win. Nobody can touch you, nobody can bother you, and no external event can harm you. You can commit suicide with it and still win! Peace of mind is all that matters and *ultimately* we all know this deep down inside us. But how can one be at peace when he or she sees someone else "ahead" of them when they feel they deserve what they have? The fight will ensue as dueling multi-categorical score-sheets arm themselves with entitlement issues. Why does this happen? This happens because we human beings cannot tolerate or watch passively as other human beings will be able to control equilibrium energy on demand (which includes ourselves) when we feel "superior" to them. We cannot bear to be "beneath" those we feel "above." If we have peace of mind energy, we will then be in control of slightly out of control energy and can do whatever we feel entitled to whenever we want to. You see—Kings need to be Kings and will not rest until they are. Queens need to be Queens and Court Jesters need to be Court Jesters or else they too will toss and turn all night long. Peace of mind energy will set in when we get our energy needs taken care of; our ability to control all the variables for equilibrium will be so fine-tuned, so sharp, so masterful that *you **will be able*** to keep up with all the changing variables around you so that you can constantly get as close to humanly possible of what you feel you deserve in each given situation. You will be aware that the *control of equilibrium energy on demand* is always changing and your **entitlement** for it is also always changing. The Universe's variables change every day at seemingly light speed. *Aware with peace of mind energy* is your ability to *consciously* keep up with the always-changing variables in your life and make the necessary adjustments to find **entitled control** *of equilibrium energy on demand* once again. I think you will find no matter how fast you adjust; the Universe will outsmart you even faster. It's a constant battle and become *aware* of the monumental task before you. Try not to feel upset if *aware with peace of mind* energy eludes you. It eludes all of us most of the time. You are not alone. The Universe moves at the speed of light—do you?

Always remember

There are two types of *peace of mind energy*. There is *unaware with peace of mind energy* and *aware with peace of mind energy*. In order to attain *aware with peace of mind energy*, there are many pre-requisite energy forms that must be attained before one can achieve *aware with peace of mind energy*. Since this book is about the *ultimate reality*, it is noted that aware is a more evolved state of consciousness than unaware. However, one must be aware that many people do have peace of mind energy yet remain unaware. These people are equal to you as long as you do not have to battle them directly or indirectly for energy. *Aware with peace of mind energy* is superior or a more evolved state of being than *unaware with peace of mind energy. Why is this? This is only true* by virtue of the game analogy. In other words, the unaware person would have to intersect with the aware person at some point in their lives directly or indirectly and engage in a competition for human energy. When the life of an unaware person intersects with the life of an aware person an inevitable contest and struggle ensues for energy so that both lives can carry on merrily on their path (this is the true nature of *reality* since attention is being used as currency). In such a contest, these two players are now playing the same game—*reality*. Now that they've finally met, the score is tied. Aware Person 1, Unaware Person 1. For the remainder of the game now, one player has knowledge of all the rules pertaining to the game while the other one does not (for he is unaware). Therefore, it is easy to conclude that the player with the knowledge of all the rules at his disposal will have an advantage over the one who does not. It is only when the aware person plays the unaware person will his or her form of *aware with peace of mind energy* reign supreme (higher vibration of evolution—not "better") because he or she will win this game by virtue of knowing how to conquer and if necessary destroy his or her opponent. When this happens, the *unaware person's peace of mind energy* is shattered as they are now made aware and forced to confront *reality*. The *reality* blinders will be blown off by force.

Question: What's my teaching on *peace of mind energy* as it relates to suicide and self-destructive behavior?

Answer: First of all, I feel you. I feel like I was born suicidal. If I ever get to actually publish this theory and you actually get to read it then I guess I made it long enough to make some meaning out of my own suffering. You see, this whole theory came to me as I was suffering extreme constant suicidal ideation and found out through my attempts to better myself with therapy, that doctors, spiritualists, whoever hadn't a clue of what reality was. It was up to me to set the record straight and educate the world to what is really going on out here. Anyway back to you, you are in fact free to walk away from life on this planet whenever you feel you've had enough. Nobody can stop you and don't worry about what others will think or do when you're gone. You are selfish as THEY ARE and they only want you here for their selfish reasons. You listen to your own body and "fuck them" they don't understand the excruciating pain you are in. It's a battle of selfishness and that is that. Other people simply don't feel what you feel and they cannot understand that's all. People *have a different ultimately neutral destiny that's* all. For whatever reason it is not "considered" a dignified way to die (in American culture). This differs from culture to culture and time period of human history to time period etc. I firmly believe in the right to die and I'm here to say "it's okay if you need to, this teacher understands you." Be aware though, that it is the only choice in life that is permanent. You're not coming back in your present form at this present time. You will lose your current "earth suit" meaning your physical body. Also—when you read a little more of this book, these teachings will show you the reason why suicidal ideation will almost *always* eventually stop. It's a race against time basically. Can you find a way to live before the pain gets too great or not? It's all in your karmic stream and time will force it to play itself out. Now all that being said, your karmic path got you to read this book and to continue reading to this very sentence so I will say this to you:

All you are looking for is a solution to your energy imbalance, and you perceive death as *equilibrium energy* that you have *control of on demand.* You feel **entitled** to not suffer anymore. You've had enough and there isn't "enough" in it for you anymore. There may be "something" in it for you, just not "enough." You need more trial and error human energy system conditioning that's all. You need more time. Crying helps a lot too. Let it out and release it. If nothing works, then you will simply do whatever works the least worst of all your choices.

Your human systems will harden up in time. I can almost guarantee it. All you want is safety from suffering and death seems like the solution (safest place). It may or may not be—but your energy will not be lost—it will go back to where it came from—the Universe. If you are in fact able to kill yourself and have *peace of mind energy* while doing so—then guess what—you win. The Universe is **ultimately** impersonal, **ultimately** impartial, and **ultimately** neutral. The word **ultimately** is up for you to define (each second, each day, each week, each month, each year etc.). If you can't define the word *ultimately* for yourself, the Universe will do it for you—it's called death. Basically life feels very personal, but it isn't. We are just energy forms looking for our perceived fair and equal exchange that's all. During the fight, it is personal. After the fight, we all shake hands and go out for drinks. The timing of the personal to the *impersonal* is up for you to figure out. It usually happens like this. During the day (the working hours) it feels personal. Then as we retire and go to bed each evening it (life) converts to *impersonal*. Life is *ultimately impersonal* because death will define the end of you taking things personally. If you get really sick or terminally ill, you all of a sudden don't care so much about all the silly "personal" things in your life. You only want out of your suffering.

Section Two

A Matter Of Invisible Laws

Doorway Seven of reality

Teaching: The Golden Key and the Secret of Life

Dear God

Other than **ultimately** impersonal, **ultimately** impartial, and **ultimately** neutral energy do you exist? I may never know, at least not in this lifetime, which is the only one I'm counting on. If you do exist, I am trusting that you now see I have tried as hard as I could to comprehend **reality**, the **root causation** of all human conflict and suffering, and the purpose of being. If I have missed something or went astray, it was definitely not for lack of interest or searching. Either way, I want you to know I am most impressed with your creation and remain in awe of you.

Everybody is equally interested in survival without pain and suffering. This is why they do what they perceive is best for them to do and think, and I will therefore follow this universal law and do what's best for me. What's best for me right now is to sit down and write this book (or attempt to at least). The salesman sees things his way, the designer his way, the accountant his, the banker his, the baker his, the electrician his, the baseball player his, the owner his, etc. Everybody simply does what they perceive is best for *them to do at the time (self-destruction and suicide included).*

Survival is not the *ultimate* goal of man, as Scientologists and Darwinists falsely believe. **Law #1** is the goal of man:

Law #1—All human thought and action (including this book) has evolved to be one hundred percent defensive, protective, selfish, and self-serving so that one can avoid, relieve, reduce, or completely eliminate all forms of human suffering via a perceived equal and fair exchange of energy. Overall human energy balance (equilibrium) is what we seek and deserve. Human energy imbalance is the *root cause* of all conceivable forms of human suffering and *all mental illnesses.*

"When failure is not an option, success is a necessity"

The Messenger

Now that we understand *reality* a little bit better, it is now time to talk about the previously mentioned conditioned "human energy system."

Question: What is the conditioned "human energy system?"
Answer: Your nervous, immune, digestive, circulatory, respiratory, urinary, reproductive systems etc. All human systems come to earth with a genetic code and instinctual systems hard-wired into us so to speak, but once you are born—***everything gets conditioned.*** Your life is a continuous trial and error, positive and negative, "blind conditioned human energy assignment" (through the brain via perceptions). Your "blind conditioned human energy assignment" is exactly that—blind to you. You will complete it because you gravitate towards pleasure as much as possible from pain. This is all part of the nervous system basically and is how we live our lives. We do not believe there is a specific pre-destined plan for you because the Universe

(God) was/is only *impersonal, impartial, neutral energy released in the "Big Bang."* I will stick with this teaching until somebody can prove to me that God has a personality and cares one way or another about anything that we do here (on earth). *It is much more sensible to believe that* the Universe/God just set invisible and visible laws in motion that we must live by. The Universe was/is just like a coiled up spring. The Universe/God wound it up (coiled it) and released it. The Big Bang was the uncoiling of the spring; that's all. Whether or not one believes in free will, heaven and hell, God, religion, Scientology, enlightenment, or reincarnation is insignificant to me. The point and theory that overrides all belief systems and thought patterns is simple: you believe what you believe because you perceive it's best for you to believe it. It's "natural selection," as Darwin would say and is one hundred percent the *defensive, protective selfish, self-interested* nature of reality. *People are protecting their energy fields best they know how every microsecond of every day.* Darwin said the goal of every living organism is to survive and propagate into the next generation to ensure the survival of the species. As stated previously, this is not true. The goal of man is **Law #1 (we are going to repeat Law #1 a lot so be warned).**

Law #1—All human thought and action (including this book) has evolved to be one hundred percent defensive, protective, selfish, and self-serving so that one can avoid, relieve, reduce, or completely eliminate all forms of human suffering via a perceived equal and fair exchange of energy. Overall human energy balance (equilibrium) is what we seek and deserve. Human energy imbalance is the **root cause** of all conceivable forms of human suffering and **all mental illnesses.**

Let's Take A Moment And Investigate Two Systems Briefly

The Nervous System

The nervous system is what makes you experience sensation through the body. The nervous system, therefore, is activated by and through consciousness. We have both a sympathetic and parasympathetic system. This means that whatever consciousness experiences through the form called 'you' is done through the nervous system. If someone hits you, you will feel the pain. Physical pain as well as emotional pain is a sensation experienced through the nervous system. The nerves that run through the whole of your body determine your sensations. These sensations are possible through the main fulcrum called the brain cortex. The brain is a receiver just like a radio receives signals from space. Consciousness, which created the nervous system, is mostly unconscious in most people and so they think they make their own decisions and choices but in truth they act unconsciously through conditioned response. For example, someone might say something that offends your ego such as saying, "You are stupid!" then the ego is affronted and there is a reaction. That reaction is not a choice but an unconscious nervous response from conditioned ideas about who one thinks one is. "Truth" is the moment itself experienced through the nervous system as an emotion of fear, terror or guilt. The nervous system was the creation of a master craftsman (God) to bring us to the realization (recognition) of who we really are. Every feeling of inadequacy, self-consciousness and fear is the nervous system conditioned response to what you have unconsciously buried by judgment. Once you start meeting this fear through the sensation triggered by the nervous system, the present fear is brought to the NOW. The moment the sensation is brought to the NOW (as pure sensation) then it becomes automatically a spiritual experience.

The Immune System

Our health and quality of life are directly influenced by the vigor of our immune system-an intricate, interrelated defensive force made up of a trillion cells. Today many factors contribute to the general weakening of our body's defenses. The ability to protect us is both instinctive and learned. Our untrained, instinctive responses are our first defense against outside threats. Just as our instincts protect us from physical threats, our immune system inherently responds to microbial threats. This action of the immune system is called innate response. The extent of this response, however, varies according to the strength and conditioning of the immune system. A conditioned immune system produces a stronger response to a given threat than a weak or naive system. If the innate immune reaction is adequate, no additional response by the immune system is necessary.

Many times, however, our innate immune ability is insufficient against the variety of microbes we encounter daily. In these cases, our immune system has the ability to learn new skills and construct new tools to deal with these microbial invaders. These immune responses are called adaptive or acquired responses.

You may be familiar with the terms "T cells" and "antibodies." These aspects of the immune system are involved in adaptive response. Once we are exposed to an infectious agent, our bodies destroy that agent by trying to identify it and react to it. This process takes about ten to fourteen days. After we have successfully dealt with an infection, our immune system retains a memory of what it has learned about this particular microbial culprit so that the body is prepared if it attacks again. Typically, we are not even aware of the subsequent exposures to the microbe since our immune system's response is so rapid and overwhelming that the microbe has no opportunity to grow effectively. This adaptive response is the result of acquired immunity. This immune response is slow but very effective.

Just as our innate physical abilities determine the rate at and extent to which we can develop athletic expertise, so too our innate immunity greatly determines our ability to effectively develop adaptive immune response. Both response systems help to determine the level of health we have, and both are necessary to keep us healthy. By examining how the immune system uses both innate and adaptive responses, we can better understand how important the immune system is to preserving our health and what we can do to support a strong immune system.

Now the secret of life and the "Golden Key" to reality

I must now take you on a very important journey. It's kind of like going to hell and back; it's a roundtrip deal. Ready? You'll be much more aware and *stronger* if you can complete this little trip we are about to be going on. Buckle your seat belt.

Rocket: Blast off!

> "If free will does exist then I have evolved to choose to not believe in it"
>
> "If free will doesn't exist, then I have no choice other than to believe in it or not"
>
> *The Messenger*

Here we go! Free will doesn't exist

Extra, Extra Read All about it!

"Free" will is an illusion, a grand hoax on humanity

The connotations of this immediately point to the fact that "good" and "evil" are not absolute. This means they are in the eye of the beholder as the ultimate nature of the Universe and God is neutral. As you will understand later, you must ignore these truths.

"Will" exists, the "will" to survive—it just isn't "free" will. "Free" will is a very interesting concept because you have as much of it as you perceive you have. In other words you will believe you have it if it is best for your conditioned human systems to believe that you do, and the same is true if you believe you don't have it. In other words you will believe whatever is best for you to believe at that particular moment and time. One must remember that all belief and thought patterns adhere to **Law #1**. Therefore whatever you believe has evolved inside you so that you feel the best about yourself or the least worst about yourself.

Law #1—All human thought and action (including this book) has evolved to be one hundred percent defensive, protective, selfish, and self-serving so that one can avoid, relieve, reduce, or completely eliminate all forms of human suffering via a perceived equal and fair exchange of energy. Overall human energy balance (equilibrium) is what we seek and deserve. Human energy imbalance is the *root cause* of all conceivable forms of human suffering and *all mental illnesses.*

Question: What is my opinion on the matter?
Answer: Well, it is best for me to believe the following at this time: I argue that man is nothing else than a supercomputer robot that makes decisions and choices based on his or her intelligence/intuition that collect data from the conditioning of the various human systems to find, hold, and protect *entitled* energy. The assignment is to find *peace of mind energy (aware or unaware).* It is a blind trial and error "conditioned human system" assignment to get the energy one perceives that he or she is *entitled* to. We are energy machines taking inflows and giving outflows in a *zero sum game with our emotions balancing out each transaction.* All one does in *reality* is react and/or respond to the feelings inside one's own body. There is action and reaction—the zero sum game of life (human emotions and moods make it so). One simply goes where he or she is meant to go to meet who he or she is meant to meet *at that time* because of the hunt for needed energy. One must go through the process

of using one's intelligence and intuition etc.; to do what they perceive is best for them in terms of feeling best about themselves (attaining needed energy). Once the various conditioning models are in place (childhood), the model is simply a one-thing-leads-to-another trajectory in which a perceived fair and equal exchange of energy is constantly sought. I believe "free" will is in fact a grand hoax, an illusion. There is will; the survival instinct is so-called "will." It just isn't "free" will. We are all on blind, trial and error, positive and negative, conditioned human system assignments.

"Free" will implies that there are choices in life that are exactly 50/50. Once we go through the process of living, thinking, and using our intelligence/intuition **we then always see one choice as "better" or "worse" than the other choice based on our selfishness** (what feels best to us on the inside). **The choice is never exactly 50/50** once we reach the inevitable decision making time. In other words, all decisions were and are inevitable (once we go through the process of actually living).

Question: Is this how I should live my life? This is very depressing. If I don't have "free will" why should I even bother?

Answer: *The secret of life is here in doorway number seven.* Now it is time to come back from hell and back to earth. Welcome back. How was the trip? The journey is *initially* brutal and upsetting, but once you understand awareness, you will find life just as interesting, just as fascinating, and just as wonderful. This is (your life), which is **an already made movie that you rented from the Universe/God.** You only get to see one frame at a time (each second, each day)—however you define the word "frame." You see, just because we do not have "free will," does not mean we cannot enjoy the *already made movie* (our lives). This is because there are so many twists and turns, so many unexpected things that happen to us, that we couldn't possibly know the ending in advance. In order to see the ending, we have to actually live our lives, and watch our destinies unfold before us (with awe). It's quite entertaining. But that's not really the heart of this teaching. The heart of the teaching is this and is your first twist to life!

In order to capture the **SILVER MEDAL**, and the second most valuable energy form on earth—*Control of Equilibrium Energy on demand* (the most superior form of *victory energy* remember) *you must believe that you are in control! Therefore you must delude yourself into believing you actually have free will! YOU MUST ACTUALLY TRICK YOURSELF TO BELIEVE IN GOOD AND EVIL!* Once again, *entitlement* is hiding here because everyone has a different amount of energy they need in order to attain *control of equilibrium energy on demand.*

Question: This teaching is hypocritical and contradictory. How can one be in *control* when "free" will is just an illusion and doesn't even exist?
Answer: The secret of life is this: We human beings must acknowledge, honor, and respect that "free" will doesn't exist (and good and evil) and *IGNORE IT*. In other words, we must live our lives *"AS IF"* we have it. The same is true for our mortality. We acknowledge, honor, and respect the fact that we will die one day and we *IGNORE IT*. From time to time we say hello to these truths and then say goodbye just as fast. In other words, we can run but we can't hide. The truth catches up to you anyway so you might as well read it here in these teachings.
Question: Can you please explain more and clarify?
Answer: This is a very difficult teaching please remember that.

#1: You should live your life in the manner that works best for you as long as you agree to Law #1. As for me, I believe "free" will is an illusion, and I believe this to be a truth in the Universe. Even though I believe it is a truth in the Universe, I do try and ignore this fact in my daily life. In other words, I see it, I'm aware of it, I understand it, and **I ignore it.** This is extremely hard to do however and if you cannot stay in denial, you can fall into a deep suicidal sever depression. If you are on this planet, you must play the game of the illusion and that is that. For example: say you are in your living room and you have a big ugly orange box that says in bold print *FREE WILL IS AN ILLUSION. A HOAX. IT DOES NOT EXIST.* **GOOD AND EVIL ARE IN THE EYES OF THE BEHOLDER.** I suggest putting this box in the corner of the room, and simply ignore it as much as humanly possible. If you happen to see it there when you pass by, acknowledge it, respect it, be aware of it, and ignore it. Put the box in the corner and try not to think about it. But it's there and you cannot escape it being there. You cannot simply throw this box out and never see it again. In simple terms; what's meant to be is meant to be and everything happens in a one thing leads to another model. This is because there are hidden laws at work that always hold true for human behavior no matter what.

Question: Are there any other illusions like this I should know about?

Answer: Yes one more **BIG ONE. Here is the other "BIG ONE." Are you ready for it? Life is not personal. It feels personal, smells personal, looks personal, but** *ULTIMATELY* **it is impersonal. Your life's meaning is to create or procreate more or less neutral energy so that you feel in equilibrium with life. When you die—it all becomes** *ultimately impersonal.* **While we are here everything feels so damn personal—but** it is not. People are simply trying to get the energy they need to be in equilibrium with life and it is different for each person. We are simply impersonal energy machines floating around this planet interchanging with each other and our environments. Our ball of energy that we are is simply concealed by our earth-suit (our skin etc.). Whatever we leave behind when we die is ultimately neutral energy because other people will exchange with it and have their different views of it (positive, negative, or neutral). So many years from now, when someone reads this (when I die)—what I have left behind is neutral energy that I have/had released into the Universe in this form (a book). I re-configured the energy that came into me in this life and simply re-directed it outwardly in the form of these writings. Some people will find this book positive while others won't even care to read it, while others will find it negative. The hardest thing to accept in life is that all of life is ultimately impersonal. I suggest you ignore this truth and pretend as hard as you can that everything is personal—this is because "meaning" is usually derived form a so-called "personal struggle."

Question: If "free" will is an illusion, then what about morality?
Answer: This is where things get ugly for all those believe in a "good" God. Morality is clearly a man-made creation so that the people with energy (power) can best hold on to it for as long as possible because they do not desire to "leak, lose, bleed, surge or implode energy." This makes perfect sense because *any energy imbalance* is so damn painful. Do you blame them? Societies pass laws that enable the ones with power (energy) to keep their energy as long as possible and ways to make people feel guilty who have too much of it. Each culture has different laws for different crimes,

etc., but in the end it is just people with energy trying to protect their energy equilibrium on the vibration they are most comfortable on whichever way you look at it. Again, this is because we humans struggle and compete for scarce, finite, **ultimately** impersonal, **ultimately** impartial, and **ultimately** neutral human energy here on earth. We only struggle to attain the amount we perceive we *deserve* and feel *entitled* to. "Good," "crazy," and "evil" are all matters of perspective. Wars happen because of the competition for scarce, finite, perceived energy equilibrium we **all** seek. Wars happen because of clashing **entitlement** for the same exact thing—*control of equilibrium energy on demand.*

When you call someone or something "evil," you must realize that it's all a matter of perspective as it directly relates to your selfish view of "well being" (conditioned human systems.)

If you don't feel too well agreeing with me about this concept ("free" will is an illusion), then don't. I understand your viewpoint. The point is not whether or not to believe in "free" will, reincarnation, heaven and hell, the Bible or any other belief you have about anything. The whole point is for you to agree to law #1. I agree to Law #1 and since this is my book and my teachings you are reading, I simply gave you my viewpoint that "free will" doesn't exist, but I ignore this truth to the best of my abilities because I want to feel in control. I am aware that I am just deluding myself, but I ignore it almost 99% of the time. Every now and then, I simply see the ugly box in the corner of my living room and pay my respects to it, that's all.

Law #1 again

Law #1—All human thought and action (including this book) has evolved to be one hundred percent defensive, protective, selfish, and self-serving so that one can avoid, relieve, reduce, or completely eliminate all forms of human suffering via a perceived equal and fair exchange of energy. Overall human energy balance (equilibrium) is what we seek and deserve. Human energy imbalance is the *root cause* of all conceivable forms of human suffering and *all mental illnesses.*

Doorway Eight of reality

Teaching: The Contrarian's View of Spirituality & The Philosophy of Human Energy Exchange

Question: How do we go about getting this energy?
Answer: The way we get energy is to use our currencies for it—our attention, internal perceptions (mental work), and/or physical work. The easiest way to look at your energy is to just think that your attention or physical labor is your investment in yourself. The absolute easiest way to think of your energy is to just simply think of your attention span as your energy span. It gets recharged each day with sleep (energy). Energy seeps into you as you consciously pay attention to nothing.

Example: A therapist pays attention to you and you therefore owe them money (energy). The rule of thumb is this: Anytime you pay attention to anything you deserve a perceived fair/equal exchange of human energy. All human conflict, emotional and mood problems come from the perceived unfair/unequal exchange of this human energy. Everything and I mean everything is a cost-benefit analysis (with regards to human energy) consciously and/or subconsciously.

To be clear now, we use our attention as "mass/energy investments." We want a return on our investment consistent with what we subconsciously and/or consciously believe is a fair and equal return for us. The fair/equal rate of return is different for each of us due to our **entitlement** issues.

It doesn't matter what the "truth" is to you. It is only a matter of perception of what the fair/equal exchange is. If you believe you deserve more, you will ask for more. If the other party feels you deserve less, they will try to give you less. This is where and when the emotional and/or psychological battle will begin. Both parties aim for the same price—to avoid all forms of suffering. **Entitlement for the same exact thing is the dynamic at work.** This should not be a surprise to you. There is not enough energy to go around to satisfy each living thing's *entitlement* issues. Animals have *entitlement* issues to (like their food and space). Conflict in life (including all wars) is therefore inevitable, normal, and the inherent true nature of reality for human beings.

The theory of reality

Now that I've got you thinking in my language, I will make things a little easier and more simplistic. *Controlling equilibrium energy on demand* also means s*afety*. *Safety* from what you ask? To feel *safe* means to not suffer and in other words means to be in *equilibrium* with regards to *energy*.

This book is the cutting edge evolving theory about the new human condition and the true nature of reality the world has been waiting for. The theory states the laws of human energy dynamics that include the premise that all human stress, depression, guilt, anxiety, and conflict come from the ***perceived*** unequal (unfair) exchange of invisible energy. The theory put forth utilizes the laws of physics from the physical realm and translates these same laws into human beings, human behavior, and human energy. The theory clearly states that all human behavior is one hundred percent defensive, protective, selfish, and self-serving, and is done so the human in question can avoid and/or relieve all forms of suffering (self-destructive and suicidal behavior explained). "Self-destructive" and suicidal behavior is simply the desire for *safety* from bleeding or imploding invisible energy (an energy imbalance). The more we feel threatened and consequently suffer, the more selfish we become for *safety*. There are no such things as selflessness, sacrifice, martyrs, or a hero because everything a person does or thinks has the subconscious and/or conscious goal of relieving and/or avoiding suffering. **Everything is therapy, a form of masturbation, a protective shield, or a defense against suffering.**

This is one huge discovery to say the least—but it has two sides to it. Suffering comes from too little energy or too much energy. It is the imbalance that causes the pain. You must get only what you feel **entitled to**—no more, no less. The theory presented in this book explains why people act the way they do, and why life is a brutal, fierce competition for scarce, finite, **ultimately** impersonal, **ultimately** impartial, and **ultimately** neutral human energy. As states, all inevitable stress and conflict come from the **entitlement** people feel for controlling *safety* via a perceived equal exchange of this powerful invisible force.

Question: Why is the energy loss side (too little side) so much more common than the energy gain side (too much side)?

Answer: The world is an inherently *unsafe* place to begin with. Anything can happen to you at any time (terrorism, loss of job, loss of love etc.). In order to feel guilty because one has *too much* energy is hard to do because abundance of energy is such a good defense. Energy imploding only occurs in an over-abundant energy state which means one has got more than one feels **entitled to**. In other words, it is very difficult in the world we have now to feel *too safe or over-safe*.

Each person has a different equilibrium point they need in order to feel safe. **Entitlement for each person's unique equilibrium** *point is secretly controlling everything*. The reason why **control** is so vital is because even if we are currently in the "safe zone," we cannot feel completely safe unless we believe we can control its occurrence. Once again, in order to feel most in control we must pretend and act *"AS IF"* we have "free will."

Concluding Doorway Eight of reality

Even though this book talks about an inherent order to human beings with regards to energy, it is a very spiritual book meant to help people make sense of their lives and take the mystery out of why things happen they way they do. Once the reader becomes enlightened (aware) to the true nature of reality, only then can the human species evolve to a place where we can talk openly about what we are experiencing here on earth accurately. I do not believe this book is inherently "good" or "bad" for mankind, since I believe the Universe is *ultimately* neutral. I do believe our species is an evolving one and consciousness is part of the evolution process. I believe this book was inevitable so I figured if I didn't write it, someone else would have eventually so why not me? The final frontier for mankind is not outer space as many people will have you think. The final frontier is the acceptance of a hierarchical structure to mankind (peasants—Kings and Queens etc.), selfishness, self-interest and *entitlement* as a truth, and a natural, normal part of human existence. The theories presented in this book will change the way you view reality forever. *It is to your advantage to understand reality.* This book is where science, psychology, philosophy, and spirituality overlap. Being spiritual and feeling *entitled* to energy (for example a lot of money) are not mutually exclusive concepts, as other teachers will have you incorrectly believe. *You can love money, and yes still consider yourself a very spiritual person.*

Doorway Nine of reality

Teaching: The Invisible Laws of reality

Question: Is it possible to have a quick synopsis of *reality*?
Answer: There are many doorways to go through (this is number seven) but the upshot is this: We are all on a blind "trial and error" conditioned human system assignment always *initially* shooting for the highest we perceive we can go (King/Queen status etc.). Let's keep this simple here and just talk about one of the human systems we speak of—the nervous system. As we go through life, our nervous systems get conditioned through trial and error as to where we fit in on the hierarchy of life. Kings will end up *feeling safest* with queens and those just below will end up feeling safest with their equals etc. Each person needs to **ultimately** accept and come to peace (*peace of mind energy* is what we want remember?) with where they fit in on the hierarchy. This is simply because if we *over-step or under-step* our **entitled** level, the Universe will step in and force you to bleed or implode energy until you submit to your rightful place. The whole trick is accepting where you fit in and coming to peace with it. Not an easy task to say the least. **You must play the vibration level that you are currently on as equally as humanly possible.** Be aware that your vibration level is always changing (you can lose or gain energy etc.).

Awareness of reality (this book) is the best defense. There is the material world that we all know about, but it is the invisible energy world that rules mankind and all living things.

The Invisible Laws of Human Energy Dynamics

Law #1—All human thought and action (including this book) has evolved to be one hundred percent defensive, protective, selfish, and self-serving so that one can avoid, relieve, reduce, or completely eliminate all forms of suffering via a perceived equal and fair exchange of energy. Overall human energy balance (equilibrium) is what we seek and deserve. Human energy imbalance is the **root cause** of all conceivable forms of human suffering and **all mental illnesses.**

Law #2—Life is a fierce and brutal competition for scarce, finite, *ultimately* impersonal, *ultimately* impartial, and *ultimately* neutral human energy. Awareness of reality (such as this book) is almost always *initially painful*, but in time ends up being *the best defense.* **Everything one does in life is a defense to acquire control of equilibrium energy on demand.**

Law # 3 — The realization that a condition previously unknown in the universe is **the root cause** for all conflict, stress, guilt and anxiety between people including all wars. This condition is bleeding (losing) or imploding (gaining) invisible energy. People are fair creatures, and only desire a perceived *equal* exchange of energy. *"Equal"* is in the eyes of the beholder, and this is where **entitlement** issues and all conflict is hiding.

Law #4 — Energy bleed or implosion is consistent with all the laws of physics as they pertain to energy in the physical universe.

Law # 5 — Subconsciously and/or consciously, all human

beings feel they have an inherent right (*entitlement* defined) to *safety or the hope of safety*. The way *safety* is attained is through a perceived equal exchange of scarce, finite, **ultimately** impersonal, **ultimately** impartial, and **ultimately** neutral human energy. *There is not enough energy to go around to satisfy each person's different levels of entitlement for safety. Conflict is inevitable.*

Law #6 —*Attention, internal perceptions, and physical work* are the currencies we use to acquire all other forms of energy.

Law #7 — Our attention (energy), internal perceptions (energy), and physical work (energy) are finite because we know we will die one day, and we know *everyone cannot be a King or Queen*. Energy on earth is finite. Our internal perceptions equal stored up energy (pent up energy). This energy has condensed inside us (not yet released), and originated from society and/or the Universe. The pent up energy goes back to where it originated from when we die (society and/or the Universe). In other words, internal perceptions create mass inside us. There is a hierarchical structure to mass.

Law #8 — The various human systems such as the nervous system can all be conditioned and make life a "zero sum game" because our systems are in effect energy-balancing machinery. Example: A boy kicks a soccer ball on a penalty kick. He scores. He gets happier while the goalie gets sadder. Here is the cosmic accounting:

Perceived equal exchange of energy = acceptable or pleasurable feeling

More than a perceived "equal" exchange of energy (over-abundance, surge, implosion, or more than one feels ***entitled to***) = guilt. One can actually have an energy aneurysm.

Less than a perceived "equal" exchange of energy = very painful feeling = *"energy leak, loss, or bleed condition."* One can actually hemorrhage energy.

Law # 9 — Human energy exchanges create all emotions and moods. Faulty brain chemistry and/or chemical imbalances are *forever outlandish improvable theories.*

Law # 10 —Life is a battlefield for the energy we speak of. Make no mistake about it—it is war. All human stress, guilt, and conflict are about the perceived unequal exchange of this very prized and precious resource.

Law # 11 —Revenge of the so-called "Narcissist." Everyone is a so-called "narcissist." When people call other people this name they are doing so because they are themselves are being narcissistic to protect themselves in order to feel better about who they are. It's a question of degree that's all. There is nothing wrong with a Narcissist protecting and defending his or her need for perceived energy equilibrium. Narcissists are an abused, misunderstood segment of our population. The entire psychiatric industry has completely missed the boat on this condition. Narcissism is another term for "feeling threatened" and/or "perceives danger" via a loss of human energy. The so-called "narcissist" will fight back and either stop paying attention to you (walk away etc.) or force you to pay attention to him or her. Calling someone a snob, elitist, or a "Narcissist" is simply your defense towards a person who is simply playing with life on a **higher vibration than you are.** That's all.

Law #12 —Energy is never lost and tends to condense before it releases (like an avalanche).

Law # 13 —There are in fact "energy classes" of people. This is somewhat similar to the old Hindu caste system but can change moment to moment. In a theoretical social vacuum—only like energy classes can exchange fairly.

Doorway Ten of reality

Teaching: Revenge of the Narcissist, The Narcissistic Answer

First of all everyone is a so called "narcissist." There are only two variables in so-called "narcissism." Number One is the fact of how highly do we score on the multi-categorical scoresheet and consequently how much human energy do we in fact secretly feel entitled to? Were we raised to feel entitled? Were we able to do whatever we wanted whenever we wanted? If so then our conditioned human energy systems (nervous system etc.) got used to feeling superior to others. Are we from a blue-collar family or executive/professional/white collar family etc.? Number Two—no matter your score or your entitlement—how threatened is your over all sense of well-being. The more we suffer and feel threatened the more selfish, "narcissistic" and aggressive we become. This is our normal and natural survival instinct and is not a mystery. People who actually call other people "arrogant," "elitist," or "narcissistic" are hypocrites because all they are doing is being narcissistic **THEMSELVES** as protection to the so-called "narcissists." This is the masturbatory nature of reality whereby putting someone else "down" makes one feel better about him or herself. What keeps getting missed in all this verbal warfare is that there is in fact, in reality an inherent hierarchy of energy that people have. For some reason, it is always left out of the conversation although it secretly permeates our entire subconscious thought (better looking people have more energy than their uglier counterparts for example in this one category). Why is this reality? Because society pays money, yes real money and **MONEY IS THE 2nd** most powerful form of energy remember to have sex with "better" looking people. The market determines who is considered good looking and who is not. People are always in a constant fight for energy and the inferior person in defense of the superior person will always end up calling the superior person "bad names" to equal out the exchange in their own inferior minds. People are selfish creatures and it really doesn't matter if they are seemingly helping other people because in the end (ultimately) it's their feelings that are driving their actions. Mother Teresa selfishly helped orphan children in Calcutta, India not because she was "selfless" but because she found a way to feel good about herself that *happened to be* helping children in India. The real mystery in life is how or why this book being written is new news to anyone. Nobody on this planet should be surprised by the words written here. If you are in protest of this book and believe it is "all wrong" then great you are **entitled to** your selfish viewpoint. In other words, go ahead and try and make yourself feel good about yourself by refuting me. I look forward to your book refuting what I say. Anyway back to Mother Teresa, all her "good deeds" were just a by-product, an offshoot of her own selfishness. So everybody is doing the same exact thing on different levels via different methods—trying to feel best about themselves or least bad about themselves. The "Narcissistic Answer" is this. In order to actually live this life one must actually like oneself. This means as soon as an external event loses interest for us we all inevitably think about our Self. We all do it. When we become bored and disinterested in the external stimuli we by default try to relieve our suffering by trying to figure out what is best for our Self. The trick is this. Be interested in yourself and everything that happens to you. Your daily diary is the most interesting book ever written and thinking only about yourself when you are bored is fascinating. Instead of self-loathing about your Narcissism and complaining about being bored, simply find thinking about yourself to be interesting. This is a foolproof way of never being bored because your life is interesting. The jail or psych ward you were in fascinates you. All your problems are interesting. Figuring out why you do what you do, when you do it, is pure narcissism. Narcissistic self-absorption or self-interest is wonderful. Everyone does it to different degrees. The less we suffer, the less we do it. We all do it when we suffer and the more we suffer the more we do it. If you spend all your money on therapy talking about yourself, then the least you can do is find it fascinating. *Ultimately* your best friend is you and talking with him or her is your best way of staying interested in life. As stated, "narcissism" comes in varying degrees because it is correlated directly into what we find interesting and what we do not. In other words, once our interest in the external stimuli dissipates we by default, think of ourselves and how to make ourselves interested in life again. It's not a disorder—it's our normal survival instinct taking over. So-called Narcissists find themselves more interesting or superior to the external stimuli they are confronted with more often than "normal" people and therefore only think of themselves. We all do the same thing when we find no external interest. The key to escaping the pain of boredom is to find your Self interesting. Your life no matter where it brings you is *ultimately* impersonal, *ultimately* impartial, and *ultimately* neutral. Just listen to your body and go where you are meant to go with fascination of the journey. In other words—be a raving narcissist. It is all of our answers. The answer is within us—to love ourselves in ourselves and to love the journey we are on no matter what the twist and turn. Narcissism is not an illness. When someone appears to be more "narcissistic" than you, he or she is protecting and defending their energy from you that's all. Guess what—they are entitled to do so, because energy imbalance syndrome is extremely painful. Can you blame them? Is it their fault that they feel superior to you? Is it their fault they were born into a certain family and you were not? *Ultimately* no one is responsible for his or her actions and you should respect this truth. We all do what we do to feel best about ourselves, it is just the so-called Narcissist is on a higher vibration than you are. In fact, we are all equally narcissistic in that we all desire our entitled perceived fair exchange of human energy. We all adhere to **Law #1.**

Go with the flow

This book is an evolving theory and breakthrough for all people suffering from conflict, guilt, stress, and anxiety. This book is a must-read for all interested in what causes human moods, emotions and all wars. A guy or girl says, "I'm from so and so place; I'm intelligent and well educated; my father does this and that; I believe and told I'm attractive; I've got all these nice things and I feel different to most everyone I meet. I cannot function "normally" because I never want to go out and socialize because there are no guys or girls similar to me, worth it or my equal. I think everybody else acts strange or just plain retarded. I just don't understand it. I don't like people, but need people. I also feel my job is beneath me and there is not *enough* "in it" for me. All this anxiety I have causes me to isolate. Then when I isolate, I feel depressed, meaningless, worthless, and get even more anxious and upset.

Question: Is this a chemical imbalance/brain chemistry problem like the doctors say it is?
Answer: The answer is no. When we search deeper—the correct ***root cause*** is a human energy imbalance on the deficit/leakage/loss/bleed side. This is a revolutionary new approach to explaining all conflict, stress, and anxiety in mankind. Once this person knows what he or she actually has, will help finally be on its way because awareness (enlightenment) is step one *and the best defense to life.* This book is that life preserver you have been waiting for as you become aware that you are not alone. This book will explain why human energy dynamics is the revolutionary theory behind the new discovery of "energy deficit/leakage/loss/bleed condition." In short,

this book explains the way the world really works. For the remainder of this book, we will simply call this condition energy imbalance condition or unequal energy exchange condition. We must always remember that too much energy is just as harmful and just as dangerous as too little energy.

Why this book?

#1 A need to announce to the world the discovery of a condition previously *unknown* by therapists and doctors is the *root cause* for depression, anxiety, guilt, and all conflict between people. This condition is hereby called *unequal energy exchange condition.* Other names we could've used include "equilibrium human energy **entitlement** condition," "abandoned prince or princess syndrome," or "dethroned, overthrown, and/or overruled dictator/emperor/King/Queen syndrome."

Also, I felt an ***impersonal*** need to publicly announce that we all carry around visible and invisible score-sheets. I am just ***The Messenger.*** Once again a modified version of what makes a person, a person:

Self-Perception	Rank Yourself	How Important is Category In Your Internal Perception	Human Energy Class: A, B, C, D, E etc.
CATEGORIES	% (Percentile) of society	Amount of *ATTENTION* you receive from . . . . *THE ENERGY STANDARD* defined previously This is the condensed energy (mass) you give yourself by your internal perception of yourself. How much attention will you get from . . . . *THE ENERGY STANDARD?* defined previously	Internal Entitlement Feelings
	1-100	1– infinity	
Your Intellect	99 X	490 =	48510

ENLIGHTENMENT THROUGH ENTITLEMENT | 113

Your Family Tree	86	X 340	=	29240
Your Grooming	86	X 450	=	38700
Your Parent's Power	90	X 200	=	18000
Your Children's Power	28	X 200	=	5600
Your Hobbies	80	X 123	=	9840
Your Creativity	99	X 490	=	48510
Your Appreciation of The Arts	40	X 23	=	920
Your Lifestyle Needs	88	X 490	=	43120
Your Physical Strength	50	X 233	=	11650
Your Physical Health	89	X 240	=	21360
Your Mental Health	89	X 400	=	35600
Your Spirituality	99	X 400	=	39600
Your Awareness	99	X 480	=	47520
Your Name	85	X 120	=	10200
Your Peer Group Power (friends)	85	X 345	=	29325
Your Wealth	50	X 480	=	24000
Your Sex (male or female)	50	X 250	=	12500
Your Breeding	89	X 433	=	38537
Your Present Address	89	X 400	=	35600
Your Address Where Raised	99	X 400	=	39600
Your Education	89	X 400	=	35600
Your Credentials	85	X 400	=	34000
Your Lineage	89	X 400	=	35600
Your Present Income	85	X 400	=	34000
Your Economic Class	80	X 400	=	32000
Your Socio-Economic Class	40	X 480	=	19200
Your Social Status	88	X 400	=	35200
Your Accent	50	X 400	=	20000
Your Ability to be Well Spoken	89	X 480	=	42720
Your Race	89	X 250	=	22250
Your Charm	99	X 400	=	39600
Your Confidence	99	X 400	=	39600
Your Perceptiveness	85	X 344	=	29240
Your Intuition	85	X 250	=	21250
Your Grace	50	X 345	=	17250
Your Rhythm (dance etc)	50	X 250	=	12500
Your Physical Beauty	89	X 490	=	43610
Your Sexual Orientation	89	X 250	=	22250
Your Coordination	99	X 250	=	24750
Your Manners	89	X 400	=	35600
Your Refinement	85	X 400	=	34000
Your Sophistication	89	X 400	=	35600
Your Book Smart	85	X 125	=	10625
Your Street Smart	99	X 345	=	34155
Your Etiquette	86	X 300	=	25800
Your Athletic Ability	86	X 50	=	4300
Your "Worldliness" (How well traveled you are)	90	X 400	=	36000
	28	X 400	=	11200
Your Cultural Knowledge	80	X 400	=	32000
Your Sex Appeal	40	X 490	=	19600
Your Personality	88	X 400	=	35200
Your Fame	50	X 400	=	20000
Your Expertise	89	X 400	=	35600
Your Coolness	89	X 250	=	22250
Your Accomplishments	99	X 489	=	48411
Your Specialized Knowledge	99	X 460	=	45540
Your Occupational Status	85	X 480	=	40800
Your Occupation	85	X 450	=	38250
Your Basic Common Knowledge	99	X 400	=	39600
Your Nationality	86	X 250	=	21500
Your Style (clothes, hair etc)	56	X 400	=	22400
Your Taste	90	X 400	=	36000
Your Personal Habits	28	X 350	=	9800

Your Personal Hygiene	80	X	250	=	20000
Energy Class Total Score	Entitlement Feelings for market rate for "human energy" = 1,862,783				

Guilt

Oddly enough *guilt* is created through both sides of the energy exchange equation. On the "more than one feels *entitled* to" side—this is the definition of *guilt*. On the "less than one feels *entitled* to" side—society makes the person feel *guilty* for wanting what he feels **entitled to**. The internal conflict to erase guilt is fierce because one has to feel **more entitled** to something than he had previously. He or she must come to terms with the fact that are more *deserving* than others will have you believe. This is because others try to defend their energy and when one feels more **entitled** to more energy than the next one, the "who does he or she think she is" conflict will begin. Society fights to keep more **entitled** people in check until an inevitable breaking point (conflict) or "mental illness" surfaces or ensues (on some level).

This condition can be fatal and is serious medical condition that nobody wants to admit exists until now! The doctors and therapists will all say the same silly things: "you're **entitled** to nothing," "you may have a brain chemical imbalance or brain chemistry problem which may be causing your root depression," "happiness comes from within," "you have to will yourself to have better thoughts" and "you're too external etc."

"That'll be $175 please."

The reader must understand that doctors and therapists are also human beings and need to defend and protect their energy. They have their own deep, dark, subconscious/conscious **entitlement** issues to deal with. *Everything* in life revolves around the secret force controlling everything—***entitlement for*** *control of equilibrium energy on demand.*

#2 The truth of the matter is and in accordance with the *laws of physics* as they pertain to energy: consciously and/or subconsciously people feel they have an inherent right to *safety* via a perceived "equal" exchange of scarce, finite, **ultimately** impersonal, **ultimately** impartial, and **ultimately** neutral human energy.

"Life is not for relaxing or even living, it's for fighting and for wars" Ultimately *Impersonal Energy*
We will discuss many interesting theories and philosophies here. These theories will contradict a lot of spiritual teachings you have heard. We will contradict such famous teachings as "all is one," the virtue of selflessness, the idea of "good" and "evil," the existence of "free" will, the ideas of Scientology, the idea that freedom and liberation come from dissolving or transcending the fears and desires of the ego, and the Buddhist notions that there is a disparity between the way you perceive things and the way things really are, and that all suffering comes from desire. We argue that all suffering comes from *perceived* unfair (unequal) exchanges of human energy.

Question: What is a perceived fair and equal exchange?
Answer: A perceived "fair and equal exchange" is different for each person and is based on his or her entitlement issues. Each person needs different amounts of energy (quality and quantity combination) in order to feel *safe*. **Enlightenment through Entitlement** contains esoteric secrets that currently have never been revealed in this world. Drawing on real life experiences, this book will tell you how to make sense out of everything that happens in your own life right now, and lets you understand why things happen the way they do (and why your moods are the way they are). Hopefully this book will be passed from hand to hand, from friend to friend. This book explains life as it really is, and explains how the true nature of reality is based on the theory of human energy dynamics (perceived fair and equal exchanges of human energy), and each person's unique undercurrent feelings of *entitlement for safety or control of equilibrium energy on demand.*

Question: Is it Nature, Nurture or Both?
Answer: The answer to this debate will now end. The answer is that life is one hundred percent societal conditioning otherwise known as societal nurturing. You are a product of your environment, your genetics and DNA, physical appearance all work in harmony to condition your internal perceptions of yourself, what you feel you deserve in life, and is how your all your human energy systems get conditioned. It is a trial and error blind human energy assignment to relieve, reduce, avoid, or eliminate all conceivable forms of human suffering. Free will is an illusion as invisible laws are at work in a selfish one thing always leads to another model/trajectory of life we are on.

Why suicidal thinking should almost always end in time

In time, you will simply learn through trial and error what hurts the least relative to everything else. Re-conditioning one's human energy systems (basically the nervous system) takes a very long time. It's a race against time to see what will win out. You will either learn how to live through trial and error conditioning or the pain will win out first and you will in fact kill yourself. The dynamic of time is the only variable that can stop a suicide, not medication that alters faulty brain chemistry or chemical imbalances in the brain. Giving medication does buy time and this is the only reason why anti-depressants work because it gives patients the hope of time. They say, "it takes six-eight-twelve weeks" for the medication to start working. Pills can relax you and I do not refute those.

Time is the key ingredient as your human energy systems have to trial and error their way through the labyrinth of life. The assignment is blind and you will inevitably selfishly pick the path that hurts the least or feels the best to you. Suicide may be your path on earth and there is nothing anyone can say or do to stop this path. It simply was meant to be this way and no other way. What are words for when no one listens to you and no one really cares *ultimately*? Do you hear me? This is the mind of a suicidal person. They/ we are in severe pain and we want to be heard and/or get out of their suffering. So I represent you. Your path is your path and will not be judged. It is not anyone's fault—it's just a one thing leads to another karmic trajectory of too much misery—for whatever reason. The struggle for mere existence was/is too great to bear.

Before you make up your mind about any spiritual issues, you owe it to yourself to see and hear both sides of the coin. Pretend it's a court of law, and I am the lawyer for my theories, the others are lawyers for their theories. Then simply decide what agrees with you and let your assignment move forward. I challenge all other great thinkers of our time to an open debate on the *true nature of reality*.

Before any debate all great thinkers will agree to law # 1

Law #1—All human thought and action (including this book) has evolved to be one hundred percent defensive, protective, selfish, and self-serving so that one can avoid, relieve, reduce, or completely eliminate all forms of human suffering via a perceived equal and fair exchange of energy. Overall human energy balance (equilibrium) is what we seek and deserve. Human energy imbalance is the **root cause** of all conceivable forms of human suffering and **all mental illnesses**.

Enjoy and welcome to all self-help enthusiasts and seekers!

Question: What do all conflicts, big or small decisions such as why and when to do something, which nation to go to war with, whom to wed, what job to take, what to do Saturday night, and where to go to dinner all have in common?
Answer: *perceived exchanges of human energy.*

Each person or nation may have his or her own personal criteria for the fair exchange, but neither nation nor individual is immune to this immutable law of the Universe. Think of your last disappointment—a broken marriage, a bad investment, a not enjoyable dinner out, and you will see the truth of what is written here.

There comes a time in life when we must all face the hard fact that some people feel "superior" to us and feel *"entitled"* to more. We call these people impolite, arrogant, elitists, snobs, or narcissists. We say they have some sort of disorder—most notably psychosis or narcissistic personality disorder. We do this because it makes *us* feel better. This book is a spiritual journey into this fascinating topic and along the way we will discover together some fascinating truths about the theories behind the laws of "human energy dynamics." This book is meant as a guidebook so that people all over the world can make sense of their lives and understand the *root cause* of all conflict, stress, and anxiety in mankind. This is a self-help book most of all because its aim is to *enlighten* people to what is causing all this tension and conflict in our species. Once we know and understand what the *root cause* of all human conflict is, we can finally begin to evolve as a species by virtue of awareness. Conflict is inevitable—nation vs. nation, king/queen vs. challenger etc. The world is now ready for a book like this to emerge because of the inexplicable events surrounding September 11, 2001, and all the conflicts surrounding "freedom," and "weapons of mass destruction." The *root cause* of every conflict and mental disorder is always the same. Clashing *entitlement for the same exact thing—safety energy otherwise known as control of equilibrium energy or the control of the hope for equilibrium energy.*

Einstein often wondered if a "grand unified theory" would ever surface for the laws of the physical Universe. A "grand unified theory" for the invisible Universe is hereby presented:

The human species is an evolving one and it has become clearer now that some invisible forces are at work. No one seems to be able to make any sense out of all the crazy events that happen in their lives. Generations have come and gone and still no one has been able to fully explain accurately what the heck is going on. Mystics, sages, scientologists, spiritual leaders, and prophets have all come and gone, only to come up empty. People all over the world are scratching their heads in utter bewilderment as to the events that are now unfolding in their lives. Now, more than any other time in history, is total confusion and chaos the norm. War seems likely to break out at any second anywhere on the globe.

This book is a theory that explains all the great mysteries of mankind.

Doorway Eleven of reality

Teaching: The Shawshank & Narcissist's Redemption

This teaching requires knowledge of the movie "Shawshank Redemption." There are many things we can learn about this movie that are quite relevant to the teachings. First of all, most people think this movie was about the power of hope and on the surface that is a fair statement. However, the movie, as it pertains to these spiritual teachings has to do with condensed energy, narcissism, and all the varying degrees of what people feel on the inside. You see, the "miracle" of/in the movie was not that Tim Robbins (Andy) chiseled through that wall in nineteen years. The miracle of the movie was that he **kept it a secret**. He told no one, not even his best friend Morgan Freeman (Red). He was holding a lot of energy to himself, which is very hard to do because energy tends to condense and then release. It is very difficult to hold onto so much condensed energy without leaking it (telling someone). The more years he chiseled that wall away, the harder it was in theory to not tell anyone. You see a narcissist is holding condensed energy (internal perceptions) much the same way Andy held his secret of what he was doing each night to that wall behind the poster. Each day that passed, the more condensed energy he held. The more condensed energy he held, the more likely he would have been to have a breakdown if he were caught. You see, a superior person simply has more condensed energy than another and therefore feels they have "more to lose" if wasted. Can you imagine chiseling through that wall for nineteen years and telling no one! Not even your best friend! You see, narcissism or feelings of entitlement/superiority are a secret that many must keep within them. It's simply condensed energy (internal perceptions) that we (them) do not want to waste.

Two more examples

Terrorist

Another example would be the feeling of holding an atomic bomb in one's trunk. Obviously if a regular person were to go through customs with nothing to hide, he will not be nervous. However, if someone has something so powerful, so dangerous, and so secretive he is hiding (condensed energy), this person will have "more to lose" if it is lost or if they are caught. This dynamic of holding condensed energy is a feeling missed in conventional psychiatry, psychology, sociology, and spirituality. The feeling of feeling superior to another is a real feeling and makes sense when we look at our feelings and emotions as being rooted in energy condensations, energy exchanges, and energy imbalances.

Precious Jewels

There are two identical men in the park. They both are dressed the same etc. It is say twelve noon. One has nothing in his pocket while the other has $5,000,000 of precious jewels in his pocket (his entire life savings) that are not insurable. Both want to take a nap on a park bench. The man with nothing to lose will not be nervous. The one with everything to lose will be. The odds of being robbed are exactly the same.

Question: Why is one man nervous while the other is not?
Answer: While the odds of being attacked and robbed while napping are equally slim, the man with the

$5,000,000 is holding more condensed energy and therefore has "more to lose." In other words, he is like a so-called "narcissist" in this situation because internally he feels more valuable than the next guy. It always comes down to condensed energy and internal perceptions of who has what "to lose." That is all narcissism is and it is incorrectly thought of in an unenlightened society as a disorder or illness. It is a personality that feels superior to another due to perceived internal perceptions which creates internal mass or condensed energy.

Doorway Twelve of reality

Teaching: $E=mc^2$

Hybrid Energy = released and condensed energy. The (E) and the (m) in $E = mc^2$

Condensed human energy (internal perceptions) can also be considered mass (m) in the famous $E = mc^2$ equation. In fact, before the Big Bang all the condensed energy (internal perceptions) that could ever be on any planet in any Universe was invisibly there. Remember this book pertains to the invisible Universe with regards to energy. With regards to energy and the formation of the Universe, one could argue that it is infinite and/or finite. No one can prove if the Universe is finite, infinite, or both. With regards to planet earth, it is finite.

Question: Why is condensed energy with regards to human beings and planet earth finite?
Answer: Firstly, we know we will die one day. Secondly, when internal perceptions on earth get too high (all living livings alive at the same time), clashing *entitlement* for safety will occur. In simple terms, everyone cannot walk around believing he or she to be a King or Queen. It just won't work. If we look to the Animal Kingdom, all species have a pecking order. **Conflict and wars are therefore inevitable since each person is shooting for a "better" way of life. Better has to**

eventually be checked and balanced by another who then keeps rising until checked by another etc. So on and so forth. Eventually each person will realize where they are "meant" to fit in and reach a state of this is "as good as it gets" and learn to accept their position.

Real World Example

The point is this—in theory, if each person were thrown at a brick wall at the speed of light squared (c^2) we would all do different amounts of damage. The elements in the Universe all have different amounts of mass. In plain English this means there is a hierarchical structure to mass (chemistry's periodic table of elements). Therefore, we conclude, there is a hierarchical structure to all of reality including people. People have different amounts of mass or condensed energy (quantity and quality of internal perceptions).

Real World Example Check

A motorcycle crashes into a wall at 30 mph, 300 mph or 3,000 mph. Obviously, the faster it goes—the more damage is done. Now keep the speed constant—say the speed of light squared. Now crash instead of a motorcycle, a car, a bus, and then a tank. The more massive the object, the more damage is also done when we keep the speed constant.

E = released human energy and m = mass = condensed human energy (internal perceptions)

Theory: E (released human energy) = m (mass or condensed human energy) c^2 (constant)

Question: What then is the constant, the c^2?
Answer: The answer is *all* human behavior is *always* defensive, protective, selfish, and self-serving. In other words,

everything we do or say is to avoid and/or relieve psychological and/or emotional suffering (bleeding/imploding energy remember). The more we feel threatened, the more selfish we become. If we bleed/implode enough energy, the hypothetical destination of death looks *safer* than living (suicide). All human behavior, "self-destructive" or not, is the selfish desire for *entitled safety* from an energy imbalance. Drinking, smoking, drugs, suicide etc. *Everything*. This is now clear. The passage of time is also part of the constant.

What is the E (released human energy)? The E = power and influence you have in the world.

So now we have in human energy terms:

$$E \text{ (released energy)} = \text{mass (condensed energy)} \times c^2$$
(selfishness for *entitled safety*).

The E (released energy) = attention (mental work) and physical work you will receive from the world. The more E, the more *ultimately* impersonal, *ultimately* impartial power and influence you have in the world. The E is *ultimately* impersonal, *ultimately* impartial, and *ultimately* neutral so *ultimately* there are no such things as "right," "wrong," "good," "bad," or "evil." True and false exist, and have very different meanings than "right," "wrong," "good," or "evil."

My condensed energy/mass inflows:

(1) I grew up in Manhattan, New York City; (2) I'm 4th generation in my family's business; (3) I belong to many exclusive social clubs including Mensa (top 2 percent IQ society); (4) I have a BBA from Emory University, went on Semester at Sea, and have an MBA from Fordham University; (5) I am told and believe I am slightly better than average attractive; (6) I have been to over 35 countries and 38 states (Puerto Rico twenty times).

Now, all that being said . . . you might be wondering why does all this superficial stuff matter? The answer is it does because of the laws of physics, which are coming a bit later. So hold off on your judgments of "superficial things" because they do matter as it relates to your total human system conditioning (what you get used to and the patterns in your life), condensed energy/mass, released energy, expectations, different levels of *entitlement for safety*, and human energy imbalances.

Doorway Thirteen of reality

Teaching: Perceptions

Simplified Examples of perceptions:

Event/thing	"Good" for	"Bad" for
Rain	Taxis, umbrella salesman etc.	Outdoor activities
Snow	Ski resorts, ski company, plow company	If you're on crutches, if you dislike snow
Smoking	Cigarette company	Your health some say
Drinking	Beer company, bars	Your health some say
Depression, mood disorders	Psychiatrists, Psychologists etc. Drug company	Whoever feels depressed and/or people whom the depressed person brings down.
Religion	Whoever thinks religion is "good" for you	Whoever thinks religion is "bad" for you
Cavity	Dentist	People who don't like pain
Bankruptcy	Bankruptcy lawyers, liquidators	People who go bankrupt
Divorce	Divorce lawyers	People who don't believe or like divorce
Weddings	All people employed by the Bridal industry	Singles Bars and Nightclubs, Dating Services
September 11, 20001	Supporters of the cause, those who cheered on that day etc.	People who miss the people who died. People injured etc. People who lost jobs due to this.
War	People in the war industries. People who believe in the war. Uniform companies etc.	People against the war. People who miss the people who died in the war.

From birth we have an inborn capacity for perception, for memory, for establishing representations of what is perceived, and gradually we develop symbolic thinking and the capacity for abstract thinking and intelligence. We absorb what's going on around us, our relationships with things and with people. The ego is like a computer, absorbing information, integrating it and learning how to sort out what is important from what is not; what is "good," what is "bad," what is helpful, what is damaging. We learn the control of our own body, and we gradually learn to differentiate what's inside from what's outside. And eventually, an internal world is built up. Part of this remains in conscious memory, and a large part goes into subconscious memory. The subconscious is like a reservoir of information that we don't think about all of the time, but that we have access to. Now, what's in that subconscious? The answer is all of that which the ego or self cannot tolerate in consciousness. It's just too intense; it's too dangerous, and it tends to get forbidden. The internal perceptions of our subconscious and/or conscious mind *control the nervous system and all our conditioned "human systems."*

Note: "Human energy" comes in many forms, and we use our attention, physical work, and/or internal perceptions to get it. ***Attention is the primary currency of human energy***. Physical work/labor and internal perceptions are less valuable currencies.

Question: How much human energy do you have?
Answer: Only you know—it's your attention (quality and/or quantity), internal perceptions and physical labor. How much are you worth? Since we, humans, in summation, are part of an energy class (*entitlement for safety* feelings are unique for everyone), it is important to understand this concept. As we have already begun to discuss, human energy from the energy standard is what we all compete for. The more human energy you can get form the *energy standard,* the higher your *entitlement for safety*. I'm sorry to say—it's basically everyone against everyone (hey you wanted to read a book on reality so that's what you're getting). I'm just the messenger so don't shoot me.

Question: What happens if someone does in fact attack me or shoot me?
Answer: Evidence that what I write is truth. Hurting me (visibly or invisibly) is a defense (like everything). If you love your religion, spiritual system, or psychiatrist so much then fine. Why shoot the messenger? *I didn't invent reality and it is not my fault. I am just the messenger.*

Question: Are energy forms a truth or is it a matter of perspective?

Answer: All forms of energy are in the eyes of the beholder and the order of importance is up to you (your conditioned nervous system and human systems). The *discovery of reality* includes the discovery and claim that all roads lead to *peace of mind energy* as the goal of every living human being. The theory also states that each living human being feels *entitled* subconsciously and/or consciously *to safety* from bleeding invisible energy (very common) or over-abundance of energy (very rare). But this is my opinion on the hierarchy of energy and cannot be construed as an absolute truth in the Universe. What are truths in the invisible Universe are the thirteen laws of human energy dynamics and I'll repeat **Law #1** here. In other words, everything written here adheres to **Law #1** which is the highest truth in mankind and everything flows from it.

Law #1—All human thought and action (including this book) has evolved to be one hundred percent defensive, protective, selfish, and self-serving so that one can avoid, relieve, reduce, or completely eliminate all forms of suffering via a perceived equal and fair exchange of energy. Overall human energy balance (equilibrium) is what we seek and deserve. Human energy imbalance is the **root cause** of all conceivable forms of human suffering and **all mental illnesses**.

We are all made up of condensed energy/mass, and/or released energy. We are always a combination of both types of energy, except when we are younger we are more condensed energy than when we get older (we are more released energy). Another good analogy for this concept would be as follows: Pretend you are a gas tank or battery that holds energy/mass. There are different grades of gas—93, 89, 87, 85, and 83 and different grades of battery power. There are different grades of people! Energy grade or class is your total score and your perception of yourself within the multi-categorical score sheet of condensed energy/mass and released energy. So say you are a grade C or 87 (energy class person), and you are in a romantic relationship with another energy C (87) person. This would be a good match! But energy can be gained or lost so once the balance is thrown off, tension will result.

Common Defenses

This is usually the time and place when religion, psychiatry, spirituality, and "lighten up" get(s) thrown around.

Religion, Psychiatry, Spirituality, Scientology and "lighten up" as a defense

Religion

Examples: "The Devil made me cheat." "God said it's wrong to do that." "Gambling my life savings away was the work of Satan." "God told me to do it." "America stands for the good in mankind." "She's the Devil." "He's a good guy because he's religious." "Allah is great." "Jesus died for our sins."

My comments

First of all,—if you are doing all these "good" deeds in this life to get into heaven then please be aware you adhere to Law #1 because you are selfish. If you are going around life telling people you are "sacrificing" in this life to get into heaven which you perceive as "paradise" or at the very least a desirable place (more so than hell I'm sure), then how can you claim to be "sacrificing" yourself. You are just as selfish as the next guy because your goal is salvation in heaven. The words "sacrifice," "martyr" or even hero do not exist in reality—it is just a cover-up for your selfish goal of being judged a "good" person by God with the reward being heaven. You are selfishly "sacrificing" here on earth so that your payoff comes in the afterlife that's all.

Enough bullshitting around—Jesus Christ (your role model) was a selfish human being trying to get into heaven just like you are. And even if you believe he was the "son of God" and not a human being, then he was still a selfish "son of God" because he only did what he did to show the way to salvation. He wanted heaven, as do you, and "sacrificed" himself so that he could find salvation for himself and for all that followed his so called "miracles." Please see the pre-face of this book where I talk about so-called "miracles."

Scientology

Examples: "That's your reactive mind acting up." "You did that because you're not clear yet." "Bad things happen to you because you didn't understand that part correctly." "You need to *buy* and read this and that book." "That's not what L. Ron meant when he said that." "What you did was irrational."

My comments

Who made L. Ron Hubbard the Messiah and the holder of all truth? This science fiction writer hasn't a clue of what reality is all about as he walked off with your money energy telling you how to live your life. The Universe is neutral, does not judge, and there is no correct way to live a life. All these so-called "bad things" in the reactive mind is simply your conditioned human energy systems remembering the past and how it felt. Basically and to make this simple—we are all on a blind trial and error conditioned nervous system assignment. We go where we're meant to go to meet who we're meant to meet at the time.

Spirituality

Examples: "All is one." "Remove and transcend the fears and desires of the ego." "Be selfless." "Perception isn't reality." "You need to release your desires." "Take the middle path."

My comments

Spiritual teachers such as Deepak Chopra, Dali Lama, and Andrew Cohen need to get a clue of what reality is all about. All is not one while we are here on earth; it's more like "all has an order." Number two—these people are selfishly making themselves feel good about themselves and selfishness is never uttered in these circles as a legitimate path to "enlightenment." Wanting to be "enlightened" is a selfish pursuit in its on right.

Psychiatry

Examples: "You have psychosis." "You have narcissistic personality disorder." You have a chemical imbalance and/or brain chemistry problem." "You have depression." "That's your depression talking." "I did that because I'm bi-polar."

My comments

There are no such things as "mental illnesses." It is a completely made up thing in human society so that people with energy can hold onto their energy in defense to you trying to take it from them. Labeling someone with a psychiatric disorder is energy because the patient feels a little better now that he or she can actually tell people what they have. The patient pays for the psychiatrist's lifestyle (family and mansion etc.). In reality—all that is happening is the fierce and brutal competition for perceived entitled human energy. Normal means 50.00001% of the population does something a certain way—the majority that's all.

The "lighten up" defense

"Life is an absurd joke to be enjoyed." "Life is a comedy." "Life is an absurd theater and we are the audience meant to enjoy it." "Lighten up, you take life too seriously." "You just need to relax." "It's really not that important, you take life too seriously." "You need to take life less seriously."

The "don't worry life goes on" defense

My comments

Who said so? Who died and made you the Messiah? People do in fact commit suicide due to personal misery and life does not always simply "go on." Give me all your money and your job and then I'll tell you to "lighten up" and "just relax." See how it feels.

Okay, now back to reality:

If a "C" person (say the male) were to get a job promotion, and he perceives this to be very important in his multi-categorical score sheet, he will go to C+. The woman, say, at this same time, has lost her physical beauty, and he perceives this to be very important in his score sheet. So now he looks at her as a C-. Sooner or later, if the balance does not come back, a lot of resentment will build up because of the perceived unfair exchange. Eventually if the woman is perceived to be a D+ and the man a C+, a breakup will occur because only like energy classes can exchange fairly. A D+ person can share all their love, attention, and money on a C person but the C person will feel too superior to accept this energy. When one is a C+ and the other is a C- they can still be together; it's just that the C- person will have to give more attention to the C+ person in order to keep the relationship together and be a perceived fair exchange of energy. Giving attention is the grand equalizer, and one must always remember is a "currency" of energy. Attention (quantity) just by itself is still too simple. We must get attention from who or what that we deem worthy of our attention. So the *quality* of attention is the "energy class" we speak of.

High-energy class people find that most (if not all) jobs are "beneath" them. They feel superior. They are superior because they perceive that they are. It's that simple. Let's try one more very simplified example so that this theory on the true nature of reality and human energy dynamics is clear.

A man perceives that being a doctor is extremely important to him. He is in med school and is dating a woman who he feels is his equal in the overall mix that he is at this time. One day he will receive his degree, however. This man also feels that having a very wealthy mate/partner is very important to him. Once the day arrives that he becomes a doctor, he feels that his mate is no longer "good enough" for him. What's that all about you ask? We say he changed energy classes by attaining his med school degree (credential). The woman, on the other hand, could win the lottery or inherit a large sum of money (energy) to also change energy classes to keep the balance of energy fair in their relationship.

Let's put it all together now:

What's important to understand is that *all human conflict* comes from the *perceived unfair exchange of scarce, finite, ultimately impersonal, impartial, and neutral human energy.* The goal of man (and all living things) is to be *true to his or her nature,* and his or her nature is to feel *entitled to safety.* In order to feel safe one must avoid and/or relieve *psychological and/or emotional suffering.* People perceive themselves, perceive other people and things, and perceive whether or not the exchange is fair or not. Where attention and/or internal perceptions go, energy goes. This is all based on the feelings of deservedness and *entitlement* on one's perceived rankings of the multi-categorical score sheet. The fair exchange is different for everybody and this is now clear. The good news is that man does not desire more than a perceived fair exchange of energy. This will also create suffering in the emotion we all know as guilt. *Safety is in the eyes of the beholder.* We live in a dynamic world of grades of energy. *People are not equal in the hierarchical world of energy class competition.* This is why people will say, "she married up," or "he married down" but that only pertains to one category—economic class.

Once we understand that every second of life is energy competition, and that only like energy classes can exchange fairly (in a theoretical social vacuum), will we be able to fully grasp the true nature of reality and the theory behind human energy dynamics.

In a theoretical social vacuum (space devoid of all matter)—this obviously includes all personal and religious beliefs etc:

If two people are not the same energy class, the inferior person will have to give more attention to the superior person. But the superior person won't care. The superior person's attention span with regards to paying attention to the inferior person will be so low that love, compassion, and understanding would no longer be possible. In other words, the exchange could never be fair because the lopsided attention given category would create the inferior person to feel misunderstood, *unsafe*, and unloved. The inferior person *in order to feel safe* will avoid and/or relieve psychological and/or emotional suffering, and therefore will end up defensive (psychologically speaking) by calling the superior person derogatory names. He or she will use such words as crazy, psychotic, arrogant, narcissistic, conceited, self-absorbed, and thereby condition him or herself (the nervous system remember) to not date that "type" anymore. You see the inferior person is still *entitled to safety* otherwise known in its lesser forms as love (energy), compassion (energy) and understanding (energy), and can only find that from a like energy class. The inferior person will end up seeking a perceived fair exchange from a like energy class person because only like energy classes are most able to understand each other (energy) and offer *safety energy*. The energy exchange between two C people will be fairer when both parties give equal attention to each other. To review: The "C" person can become a C+ or C-, and when this happens, the exchange becomes slightly unfair and causes tension and conflict. This gradation or nuance is not enough to cause a breakup because the variable of attention will be compensated for to create equilibrium once again.

In your "ballpark" and energy class For example picture 30 major league baseball stadiums. You are sitting in the front row. Everyone sitting in your "ballpark" is your "energy class." Those sitting closer to you are more exactly on your frequency and those sitting further away (are still in your energy class) just not a perfect exchange for you. There are nuances in each energy class, but it is important to understand that once someone is not in your "ballpark" they just aren't. Different energy class people can never exchange fairly in a pure social vacuum context. The different ballparks have breaking points to where the line drawn that differentiates our energy classes. A last row Energy A person cannot exchange fairly with a front row Energy B person and that is that.

Once energy class has changed enough from say a C+ to a B-, the change has reached a point where all the attention in the world would not make a difference because the partners could not longer understand each other (no energy).

Understanding that your perceptions of your rankings in the multi-categorical score sheet of characteristics and attributes make up your energy class is one of the foundations of the *Institute of Impersonal Energy* and theory behind human energy dynamics (theory of reality).

Human energy dynamics is quite simply the marriage of many laws of physics as they pertain to motion and energy in the physical realm to the notion that *all* humans are also made of energy and must adhere to the same principles. It is an unfortunate reality, but here on planet earth people do feel "better" or "superior" to other people based on their perception of reality. When a person feels "better" or "superior" to another, they then feel more entitled (for nice things etc.) than the other.

Warning—*more reality is coming. Initially disturbing text ahead.*

Question: What do Mother Teresa, Osama Bin Laden, George Bush, Sadaam Hussein, Adolf Hitler, Gandhi, Dali

Lama, Deepak Chopra, L Ron Hubbard, Buddha, Mohammed, Terrorists, and Jesus all have in common?
Answer: This should no longer come as a surprise to you. They are/were all selfish human beings looking for *entitled safety and adhering to Law #1*. We all do the same exact thing. **This should not come as a surprise to you. What's the big deal with admitting the truth?**
Question: Are the people we call evil aware that they are evil. Do they think of themselves as evil?
Answer: No. Evil is a matter of perspective. You just don't understand reality. Keep reading and go back and pay special attention to the illusion of free will teaching.

Human energy is scarce, finite, *ultimately* impersonal, *ultimately* impartial, and *ultimately* neutral.

Doorway Fourteen of reality

Teaching: "The Multi-Categorical Score Sheet" in more detail now

Society is the measure and created the natural order but it's ultimately how you perceive yourself. Your internal perceptions get validated or invalidated by society and the evidence mounts. Society creates your perceptions of reality, people and things, and yourself and where you fit in (peasant-King/Queen etc.).

Our old friend "perceptions" from the prior teaching is here again. **Perception is reality** and this is where I disagree with many other so-called "spiritual teachers." By the way, doesn't anybody notice how wealthy guys like Deepak Chopra or L. Ron Hubbard are/were? Internal perceptions of our rankings in the categories come about as we go through life and meet other people and the world. As we go through life, if "everybody says so" about something about us such as our attractiveness then eventually that will be our perception. So if we perceive that we are great at, say, basketball but everyone we know thinks we stink and the statistics show that we do—then our perceptions about this trait will level off at more or less where the truth is. Another example would be if we perceive that we are expert at, say, standardized tests. Then as we take them—we consistently score below the 10th percentile—we must eventually face the truth that we are lousy at these types of tests. As we get older, our internal perceptions of ourselves will intersect the truth about ourselves based on how the world receives us. So, the world's truth helps us in making our internal perceptions as close to truth as possible. We cannot perceive something completely off base about ourselves, because as we go through life these perceptions will either be invalidated or confirmed by others as we go through life. The evidence mounts for us or against us as we test out our perceptions of ourselves as we compete and hunt for human energy in the marketplace of life.

How you perceive yourself is your energy *and your entitlement level for safety energy.*

The order is natural and is bred into your nervous system as you grow up and is the secret underlying force in the universe. *People are not created equal with regards to energy inflows into the conditioned nervous system.* Some ideas are simply better or superior for example, and some people are simply more popular and beautiful etc. The multi-categorical attributes that make up this order are all the things and your perceptions of yourself that make you be you. It is the blend, the mix of things that make you who you are. One must always remember that money is energy and many of these categories are provable quantitatively and have money flows invested into them. This includes physical appearance (genetics) and sexuality. What you look like is worth energy—in this particular case, money! Especially for women, a lot of *entitlement for safety* comes from how they perceive their physical attractiveness (escorts, models, etc., do in fact *get paid*). The sexier they feel they are, the more they feel they deserve. This is only one category but a powerful one.

Conditioning the nervous system and all human systems

1. **Watch the Money Flows**—Escorts, models, and prostitutes *get paid* at different rates. This is the market for sexuality/physical appearances. This is because of the woman's sense of offsetting credentials that equal her price. For her, her credentials are her perceived physical beauty. The market

and her entitlement create her price. Her market rate can of course change in time as variables change (for example: her need for money or demand for her services.). The point of these writings is to understand that she may in fact eventually hit a "rock bottom" price. She will not go lower because she feels that going lower in price would be "beneath her" and that she's "better than that." We all draw the line somewhere (pride). What's important to understand is that we all have different prices for ourselves *for everything and reach a certain point that we simply draw the line. Our pride (ego) simply feels "id rather be dead than work at that job. It is simply beneath me."*

2. **Watch the Attention Flows**—Attention is energy. For example, better looking people (male or female) get and got more attention growing up based on this one category. "Cool" kids also get more attention and form a popular "in" crowd in school.

3. **Watch the Quality of the Attention Flows**—Attention is energy. But who was/is paying attention to you? Was "the energy standard" paying attention to you, a King or Queen paying attention to you, or a peasant? It matters.

NOTE: ** Weighting of each category is up to each person. For example: Some women rank themselves primarily on the physical categories. This is an unenlightened (unaware) view of reality.

How One Ranks Oneself = Self-Created "Energy Class"

The theoretical multi-categorical sheet				
Perception	Perception			
	Rank yourself	In your own view:		Weighted
Add or subtract	in what % of	How important do you believe		Summation
Categories as you see fit.	All people in	Category is to acquiring the		Of all
	Society	Energy of "the energy standard"		Categories
Note: If you do this with a friend or relative, you must use same exact categories.				
				Totals
Author's note: I am not judging reality as right, wrong, good or bad. I am just explaining reality.				
This book is after all about the "true nature of reality."				

Here it is again, now that you are more understanding of what it is:

The Silent Majority's Way of Judging People

Question: What is the point of the score-sheet?
Answer: The point is for you to understand that everything in life is ranked. People and things are ranked in many different categories in life by one's internal perceptions of them. *Everything in life is ranked. This should not come as a surprise to you.* The categories are up to you. If you want to know who feels more *entitled (has a higher safety level)* for human energy between you and another individual, you must agree on which categories to use. I will not list all the categories because in theory relative to the infinite Universe, they are infinite. Once again, relative to planet earth, they are finite. *We're all on borrowed time. We all have a terminal illness. It's called life.*

Once again from doorway number one:

This is how we judge people and ourselves. There is an inherent hierarchical structure to people with regards to quantity and quality of the energy that they emanate. What we desire is our perceived fair and equal exchange of energy. We feel secretly feel entitled to it.

Energy Forms that Radiate/Emanate directly from People: Things people have that are ranked in reality.

Invisible or Must Ask The Person in Question	Visible or Need Not Ask The Person in Question
Family Tree	Physical Strength
Heritage	Physical Health
Birthright	Fitness
Inheritance	Sex (male or female)

Tradition	Race
Genetics/DNA	Reflexes
Intelligence	Laugh
IQ	Voice
*Powerful Last Name	*Powerful Last Name
*Hero/Celebrity/Fame Status	*Hero/Celebrity/Fame Status
Social Breeding	Smell
Social Affiliations	Vision
Professional Affiliations	Height
Creativity	Weight
Hobbies	Body Shape
Appreciation of Arts	Smooth Skin Face
Lifestyle	Smooth Skin Back
Attitude	Smooth Skin Chest
Spirituality	Smooth Skin Arms
Awareness	Smooth Skin Legs
Religion	Hair
Peer Group	Eye Color
Address Raised	Eye Shape
Atmosphere Raised	Eyebrows
Address Present	Eyelashes
Ability to "roll with punches" in life	Eyelids
Ability to "Function"	Eye Socket (bags etc.)
Education Level	Nose Shape
Education (Schools Attended)	Nostrils
Credentials	Ears
Ambition	Ear Lobes
Wealth	Upper Lip
Work Ethic	Lower Lip
Income	Face
Socio-Economic Class	Lack of Wrinkles
Social Status	Cheekbones
Net Worth	Chin
Well Written	Head
Well Spoken	Forehead
Well Read	Arms
Charm	Elbows
Confidence	Forearms
Perceptiveness	Hands
Intuition	Palms
Grace	Fingers
Rhythm	Fingernails
Coordination	Knuckles
Manners	Shoulders
Refinement	Cleavage
Sophistication	Chest
Book Smarts	Breasts
Street Smarts	Nipples

Regal Etiquette	Stomach
Athletic Ability	Lack of or not, Body Hair (upper body)
Birthplace	Lack of or not, Body Hair) (lower body
Zodiac Sign	Lack of or not, Body Hair (back)
Multi-Cultural Knowledge	Lack of or not, Facial Hair
Humor	Upper Back
Personality	Lower Back
Expertise	Body Type
Personal Accomplishments	Accent
Specialized Knowledge	Waist
Occupational Status	Hips
Desired Occupational Status	Skin Tone
Basic Common Knowledge	Belly Button
Nationality	Love Handles
Style (clothes, hair etc)	Inner Thigh
Taste	Outer Thigh
Personal Habits	Legs
Personal Hygiene	Knees
World Travels	Shins
Popularity	Feet
Pride	Sole Feet
Charisma	Toes
Metabolism	Toenails
Sexual Orientation	Lack of or not visible veins
Actual Life Experiences	Neck
Chronological Age	Décolleté
Physical Age	Calves
Psychological Age	Ankles
Spiritual Age	Tongue
Aptitude to learn new things	Genitalia Shape
Desires	Genitalia Size
Cravings	Genitalia Functionality
Physical Needs	Genitalia Pride
Physical Space Needs	Seductiveness
Privacy Needs	Sexual Abilities
Intellectual Strength	Teeth
Mental Strength	Gums
Emotional Strength	Smile
Interesting Personality (Engaging Conversationalist)	Adam's Apple
Prior Nervous System Conditioning	Wrists
Religious Thoughts	Flexibility
Political Thoughts	Masculine
Social Thoughts	Feminine
Sexual Thoughts	Buttocks
Family Values	Dimples

Self-Esteem	Lack of or not beauty marks
Social Skills	Walk
Parental Abilities	Stance
Entitlement for nice things	Posture
Lack of or not Powerful Aura/Energy field	Presentation, Packaging, Overall Look
Body Attitude	Lack of or not Blemishes
Outlook on Life	Tattoos/Body Art
Employment Stability	Body Piercing
ADD WHATEVER YOU	FEEL IS IMPORTANT

Clashing entitlement for safety was, is, and will always be the issue and will occur when the internal perceptions of two or more living things feel entitled to the same exact thing. Wars, crimes, animal attacks etc. are inevitable because there isn't enough safety energy to go around (satisfy each living organism's *entitled safety* issues).

Some real world examples:

Basically, were you raised a Prince/Princess or a peasant?

But even this is too simple. Are you a wise, attractive prince/princess or are you a wise, ugly prince/princess? Do you leave your own little world of other princes and princesses and mingle with *the energy standard?* Are you able to connect with *the energy standard* or only other people just like you?

Are you a wise, attractive, cool, charming middle-class guy? Are you an average-looking, wise, nerdy, athletic, newly minted multi-millionaire genius man but with no taste whatsoever? Are you a very good-looking, wise, cool, athletic, slim, fit, unemployed, poor genius man but with great charm? Are you an ugly, wise, athletic, multi-millionaire man, but extremely nerdy with no sense of manners? Are you a wise, cool, extremely overweight princess genius with no taste whatsoever? Are you an ugly princess who went to all the best schools and has all the best credentials? Are you from the absolute middle of nowhere small town with zero talents whatsoever?

One can play with all the categories for a lifetime and make up an entire human being who currently has a hand dealt to him or her with scores (cards) in each category. How good is the overall hand? Are there two aces, thirty Kings, sixty-five Queens, five Jacks, and three tens etc? What is the overall mix? What is your hand like? What is your perceived market value for "human energy?"

Question: So how does one know whom the "superior" person is?

Answer: In a theoretical social vacuum (a space devoid of all matter), the person who stops paying attention to the other person first is the superior person (the one with more human energy).

Question: What if there was a person who perceived himself or herself to be a very high scorer in all the categories that matter. In other words, he or she would be perceive himself or herself beautiful, intelligent, perfect charm, perfect accent, perfect manners, perfect occupation, perfect work skills, and perfect social skills in which he or she could relate to all of mankind equally etc? Wouldn't this person feel "worth" more?

Answer: This person would want to, expect to, and feel entitled to their fair exchange of human energy and especially the most superior form *(safety)*. In fact since energy is never lost, why should this person want anything else?

The only alternative would be the very painful "energy leakage/loss/condition" which would create psychological and/or emotional suffering (all forms of human suffering). The human being would then very painfully bleed invisible energy and have their *safety threatened*. Human beings are hard-wired to fear suffering and bleeding invisible energy is tremendously painful. This is why people act the way they do. Once again, *bleeding invisible energy is extremely painful and entitlement for safety is behind everything. None of this should come as a surprise to you.*

Such a person would feel superior to most all that he or she met, but may or may not let on that he or she felt this way. Perception *is* reality. As an adult, this person would feel *entitled* to energy because *it was theirs to begin with* (mass/condensed energy, Newton's third law of motion, and second law of thermodynamics). *It was his or hers to begin* with because it had in fact condensed inside his or her nervous system. *Entitlement* is most obvious when a person is trying to reclaim what they believe was theirs to begin with, and was unjustly (meaning no fault of their own) taken away. The other form of *entitlement* is—why does so and so have this and that when I'm "better" than he or she? Why should I get less?

To keep this as simple as possible: Basically as children we condense it, then as adults we exchange with it.

Question: How does one know when they are no longer *"safe?"*
Answer: When they can no longer trust themselves *to not attempt* suicide, or they can no longer trust their environment *to not attempt* to make them feel overwhelming stress, anxiety, depression, conflict, injure or kill them.

Doorway Fifteen of reality

Teaching: Stress, Anxiety, and Conflict are explainable and inevitable

This condition invisibly permeates all societies and all people. This condition is simply a matter of the universal laws of physics and esoteric universal law about the true nature of reality as it pertains to energy—human energy. The discovery of the laws of human energy dynamics as outlined in these writings is indeed revolutionary. If you are or know someone who is often anxious and stressed, the same *root cause* is always in effect. It is not a brain chemistry problem causing emperors, dictators or presidents to act the way they do. It is clear that both sides in any war consider the other party "irrational" and/or "mad." It is clear that both sides use God as the password to the doorway of "good and evil." The same laws of human energy dynamics relate to you and I on a daily routine level. It is most apparent when a human being refuses to work or do a job that they feel is "beneath them," or will not date someone because he/she is not "good enough." Human energy is the actual force at work, not ego, and this is why this book is about the hidden laws of "human energy" dynamics not "ego" dynamics. This needs to be discussed, studied, and documented as a truth in the universe since all the *laws of physics* as they pertain to motion, energy, and mass validate the claim that energy is never lost—just transferred around. If it's not lost then where does the energy loss/gain go? The answer is that the energy transfer creates human emotions and moods. It's that simple. Energy is transferred in every interaction (attention, internal perceptions, and physical work). Everyone on planet earth can relate to the fact that sometimes we are simply unable to will ourselves into a good mood or accept our situation no matter how hard we try. All other diagnoses such as brain chemistry malfunctioning, chemical imbalances in the brain, or even personality disorders are simply all offshoots of the same primary *root* cause. The "chemical imbalance" argument for why depression and anxiety occur is *not provable*. "The exact mechanism of how antidepressants work is not known" is what every psychiatrist will say. *Then you pay them.* If we could all simply feel better by taking psychiatric pills (anti-depressants, etc.), then going to psych wards, depression, stress, anxiety, wars and suicides wouldn't occur. If we could all feel better this way, we would. A patient, who believes the pills are working, will gain energy from the pill if they trust and respect the doctor. The pills *are* the doctor(s) and we can in fact derive a lot of energy from them if we trust and respect them. But, for some of us we simply cannot feel better. Believe it or not, we may in fact *feel superior to the doctor.* We may have knowledge of a psychiatrist who committed suicide himself or simply find our doctor ugly, unintelligent, and/or nerdy. By the way—I am only refuting drugs for brain chemistry and chemical imbalances in the brain *not nervous system drugs.*

Question: If faulty brain chemistry and chemical imbalances are science fiction then what is bothering me?
Answer: The *root cause* is "human energy imbalance disorder." This disorder like all other disorders comes in all different degrees and strengths. People can in fact bleed or implode invisible energy. One can actually "hemorrhage invisible human energy." In order to fully understand this disorder one must first understand many laws of physics (which I will explain to you a little later), and discard every previously held

notion of spirituality. I will then make my case for the true nature of reality on planet earth and the laws of human energy dynamics.

The simple equation for happiness is Happiness = Reality/Expectations. This is too simple. The reason why is because of the word "expectations." This is the word we must focus our energy on because hiding beneath this word is the dirty little secret of life—*entitlement for safety*. Entitled people are at every level of society. People in all cultures, and from all different levels of society feel superior to someone else and therefore expect and feel they deserve more in life. Entitlement is probably the most explosive word this world has ever known. This one word may in fact literally blow up and destroy our entire human species if we're not careful. Entitlement for land in the Middle East is indeed explosive. My definition of *entitlement* is this and will serve as a guide for this book: *Entitlement* = people feel they have an inherent right to *safety* (not leak/lose/bleed energy). Bleeding invisible energy is an *unsafe* feeling. This is otherwise known as getting a perceived fair exchange of scarce, finite, ultimately impersonal, impartial and neutral human energy. When Ivan Pavlov offers his expert testimony later on, this point will be even clearer (yes, we will have a trial and you are the jury). The people who I will call upon during the trial phase of this book are guaranteed to startle and amaze you. Some Examples of How Energy Exchanges Cause Emotions:

Exhibit A

Energy leakages/losses feel bad (Macro-Energy)

Imagine a child who is raised as a prince for say twenty-one years (Prince William, etc.). He did nothing in life except be a good son and do what his parents told him to do. Then when he is twenty-one he becomes abandoned and is thrown into society as a peasant. He is now an incognito king/prince amongst peasants. Is it no wonder why this child/young adult is or will be depressed and feel bad? Is it a mystery? Do you really think his "brain chemistry" is causing his misery? Is it his fault that he was raised by these certain parents who could no longer "back up" the lifestyle he thought he had and became accustomed to? Is it his fault that he lacks the necessary skills and doesn't know how to earn a living in the manner he became accustomed to? The correct *root diagnosis* of his depression and misery is *"human energy leakage/loss disorder."* Wouldn't any normal human being feel terribly depressed if they were raised a certain way, expected a certain lifestyle, felt *entitled* to it, only to see it vanish one day due to no fault of their own? The theory behind this revolutionary model of the laws of human energy dynamics helps explain why leaders in countries such as Iraq and North Korea are/ were so desperate to hold onto their power. As we dig deeper in this condition, we see what is really going on and can unlock esoteric secrets that drive all human behavior. We see a human being who had *condensed energy* (second law of thermodynamics) inside him, meaning he was bred with energy and then will be "leaking" energy after the dethroning or abandonment. Human energy leakage, or fear of it, causes all of the psychological and/or emotional agitation in the universe today. Fear of the *unsafe* (energy bleeding) is behind everything. The psychiatric/mental health profession needs to be completely overhauled and understand this condition as a truth forever embedded in reality. All I am trying to do now is enlighten people as to what *entitlement* is and where it comes from. If one perceives unfair human energy exchanges currently or in the near future (feels power is threatened), they will feel upset, nervous, anxious and depressed. They will begin to fight back to get what they feel is/was theirs to begin with—energy. In a nutshell, this is why many people from old money jumped out of windows and committed suicide when they lost all their money in the stock market crash of 1929. This was a sudden and drastic loss of scarce, finite, human energy—an "energy hemorrhage." In this particular case, the energy form was money. When we look deeper, the money was what made them feel *safe*.

Exhibit B

Energy Surpluses/Gains Feel Good (Micro-Energy)

In Manhattan, New York City, all the public buses take metro cards, which is how the vast majority of us pay our fare. We can also use coins if we choose to. Everyone expects to pay the fare one way or another and then is *entitled* to a bus ride. Just the other day I was on the bus sitting near the front where I could see people's reactions as they entered onto the bus and pulled out their metro cards to pay their fare. I was watching very carefully now because I already knew what they did not—that the bus' metro card machine was broken and that the ride would be free (unless you demanded to use coins which nobody did, of course). This was also part of my research for this book (to study reality). Anyway, as each person boarded the bus (like I had done before them) they each pulled out their metro cards only to be told by the driver that the machine was broken and to *"just pass through." Each person either smiled or said "thank you" to the driver in a pleasant grateful tone.* Not one offered or insisted to pay in coins. The point is this—each person's mood was uplifted ever so slightly the instant they gained a "perceived more than a fair exchange of energy." They felt "lucky" to have gotten this particular bus at this particular time and for that split second I watched them—their mood improved. Why you ask? The answer is a perceived more than a fair exchange of energy (in this case money, *but did not feel guilty*). Once you don't feel guilty, the exchange becomes fair again and guilt is erased. Luck is also a form of energy by the way and people feel *entitled* to some of it (people have varying degrees of how much luck they feel *entitled* to). People want luck to offset and balance out their perceived "bad luck." This is why people feel *entitled* to luck. I know it's only a small amount, but hey, the theories presented in this text need to have examples, no matter how big or small.

One more quick, simple example:

In soccer, hockey, or a baseball game a player scores a goal (hits a homerun). In a *game vacuum* (meaning all other variables are taken out or made equal), the player gets in a better mood when he or she scores and the goalie (pitcher) gets in a worse mood. This is a simplistic example of an energy exchange and *should not come as a surprise to you.* Scoring goals or points in a game you care about is another form of energy.

Doorway Sixteen of reality

Teaching: Why at this time?

I felt compelled to write this book because of the wars that we are now faced with which will continue for a very long time (terrorism, etc.), and to help shed awareness on why there is in fact all this conflict in the world today. I had read many books on spirituality, attended some seminars, and even went on a retreat with a famous teacher of our time only to be disappointed time and time again. "Remove or transcend the ego" is all they can say like a stupid broken record. "How?" is all I could say. I never got an answer because it's not possible. I also looked for answers in individual therapy for my own depression, only to realize that no one has a clue as to what is really going on in reality. I sincerely hope my theories catch on and that perhaps I will be the spokesperson for it. I am indeed a human behavior theorist. I named this book *Enlightenment through Entitlement* because of two reasons. Number one, enlightenment to me just means "awareness" (though other spiritual teachers talk for twenty hours on what it means). And number two; *entitlement* is the permeating dirty little secret of all people in all societies. We must understand what *entitlement* is, and where it comes from, if we are to evolve and survive as a species. I challenge all great thinkers of our time to refute my teachings.

I hope that these philosophies and theories revealed here create a new, more complete world view in which humans can talk about what we are experiencing here on earth accurately, use the correct language to describe it, and understand that the laws of human energy dynamics are secretly guiding all human behavior. I also hope that all people suffering from so-called "mental illness" can now understand that the *root cause* of their mood problem is human energy imbalance disorder. The doctors simply have it wrong, but it is not their fault. They simply have never heard of these theories before. For psychiatric conditions caused by *obvious* physical problems (such as brain damage), these theories do not apply. However, if no physical problems are evident, the faulty "brain chemistry" and "chemical imbalance" hypotheses remain improvable (and will be impossible to prove forever). In fact, the current theories used in psychiatry, and the current teachings in spirituality *are in fact more* outlandish than my theories outlined in these writings. Doctors and spiritual teachers need to understand that people do in fact bleed and implode invisible human energy.

The timing of this book is exactly when it should be. Now is the time because cell phones and the Internet have made a complete mess out of the dating scene (and created an almost perfect human energy marketplace). This generation is different and we feel it. There is a different reality now, a new human condition. It is now clear that all people are in a fierce and brutal competition for the same thing—scarce, finite, ultimately impersonal, impartial, neutral human energy—and will not stop competing or "settle" until they get what they perceive they are *entitled* to. This exact same dynamic at work in dating also surfaces when nations square off for war.

The Universe/God/Creator (whatever you want to call it) only created neutral condensed mass and then after the explosions in the Big Bang came released neutral energy. Since nobody has ever proved that this energy has a personality, I call it impersonal, impartial, and "neutral energy." Not "good" or "evil" energy (positive or negative). In other words, this energy/mass does not care one way or the other what you do with your life. It is simply **ultimately neutral**—the way it all started (the way you came into this life is the same way you are leaving it—a neutral energy carrier. This energy/mass has seeped into mankind and is present by our births. This is what powers us—energy and mass. This is why we are not plugged into an energy source to move; we just go. Man's nervous and all human systems can be conditioned any which way and is the holder of the energy and mass we speak of. Man's first micro-millisecond on earth is in the unconditioned state (absolute). From the moment he/she is here, the nervous system etc. is being conditioned by mass and energy. The nervous system knows all and we are all on blind "trial and error" conditioned human system assignments or "ultimately neutral human energy assignments."

Society now needs to believe in something "more." There is something else going on here as evidenced by September 11, 2001 and all this present conflict. Now we will learn the true nature of reality. Now we will understand that all major world religions (including Scientology) and philosophies have it wrong. Now is the time to understand and to see that the truest nature of reality has to do with an inherent energy/mass order to human beings. People don't understand why people act the way they do. Generations have come and gone to create material comforts and to "get ahead." Then came the Internet, email, and cell phones. Technology opened up the world now so we can all ask what else is there to do? What else is there to understand? The answer is to understand the theories of human energy dynamics and the defensive, self-interested nature of reality.

The main premise of my argument is that which opposes what you hear in religious and spiritual services throughout the world each day. Each day spiritual people love to claim such silly things as "all is one," "you are neither beneath nor superior to no one," and "remove or transcend the ego." I say these are all false and misleading claims and completely off the mark with regards to reality. While it is true, before we are born and after we die, we may all be the same spirit and our atoms are of the same molecular dynamic, I prefer to stick to reality here on earth while we are alive. As you will understand later, my theories are all consistent with the laws of physics as they pertain to energy and motion. In particular we will discuss and intersect with Newton's third law of motion, Einstein's special theory of relativity, the two laws of thermodynamics (the study of the motion of energy), Darwin's theory of natural selection, and Ivan Pavlov's experiments with his very famous dog. We will also briefly mention Stephen Hawking.

SECTION THREE

A Matter Of Science

Doorway Seventeen of reality

Teaching: The Trial of Reality

Reality will now go on trial with you, the reader, being on the jury.

Question: First of all, what does "truth" mean?
Answer: Truth is not a belief or an opinion. Truth is provable objectively by all. It is a Truth that people want to feel "good" and not "bad" (if they have a choice in the matter). Also another Truth is how much money is sitting in your checking account at this very moment? We can all see the amount in there because it is based on numbers. Math and Science prove things and when many different scientists prove the same exact thing throughout the ages we call the "truths." This is because each scientist found them same thing to be true over and over again, and eventually we humans must acknowledge that they all can't be wrong (false). This is why my teachings about energy imbalances being the root cause of anxiety, stress, and conflict AND having math and science behind them, is a superior theory to the one currently used in psychiatry. No scientist has ever proven that people actually have chemical imbalances in their brain or faulty brain chemistry. The drug companies (Prozac etc.) want you to believe that to make you feel better. When you take one of these anti-depressants what you are really

connecting to is the placebo energy effect of your doctor, the advertisements and marketing for the drug, and your powerful belief that this drug goes into your brain and somehow alters your chemistry to make you feel better. Do you honestly believe feeling good about yourself can come in a pill? As improvable and implausible it is, many people believe in these pills and that's fine. All I am doing is writing about a possible different hypothesis about human stress and conflict and what its root cause is. Why can't there be two theories on the table? Mine is the "energy imbalance" theory and it will compete with the current chemical imbalance or faulty brain chemistry theory. As outlandish as you may feel my hypothesis, theory, axiom is (whatever you want to call it), I believe (and I think you will to) that my theories are in fact, much ***more provable*** and *less outlandish* than the current improvable ones.

Can anybody out there prove depression via brain chemistry being faulty or imbalanced? Where is the evidence? Show me the numbers? Where is the data? Depression has not and will not be provable via measuring ones serontonin or dopapine etc. or whatever neurotransmitter jargon bullshit "they" come up with. Chemical levels in the brain causing mental disorder is hello— NOT SCIENTIFICALLY PROVABLE. Even if you could prove this, "the law of diminishing returns" would kick in once you took a drug to feel better and make your life "what you wanted." This is the book the drug companies don't want you to read. Remember I am only refuting drugs for "brain chemistry" and "chemical imbalances" in the brain.

Question: What is the "law of diminishing returns?
Answer: In economics, law stating that if one factor of production is increased while the others remain constant, the overall returns will relatively decrease after a certain point. Thus, for example, if more

and more laborers are added to harvest a wheat field, at some point each additional laborer will add relatively less output than his predecessor did, simply because he has less and less of the fixed amount of land to work with. The principle, first thought to apply only to agriculture, was later accepted as an economic law underlying all productive enterprise.

For example—I like massages. But after about 2 hours of massaging—it doesn't feel as good anymore as the previous two hours did. The ability to enjoy something starts to diminish at a certain point in time if the agent, the variable is constantly applied. You'll want more and more, but it won't work. In other words, even the most pleasurable things on earth lose their value when we get too used to them. So in other words, even if drugs made you feel better (which I've stated is not provable), but just imagine I'm wrong and they actually do work (nobody knows how, but just play with me an imagine they do). Then what? Now you're "feeling better." Now what? You'll want to eventually feel better from "feeling better." And then feel better from feeling better once again. So on and so forth. The feeling will wear off as you get used to "feeling good." The only way someone knows what "feeling good" is to compare it to "feeling bad." It's all about energy inflows and outflows and nothing to do with brain chemistry or chemical imbalances. Psychiatric drugs for depression miss the entire picture of what human reality actually is. They miss the competition for human energy as the root cause for all human suffering. Amen.

The scam of all scams—depression, manic-depression etc. caused by faulty brain chemistry and/or chemical imbalances in the brain. This is the book the Drug Companies and the psychiatrists don't want you to read!

Next time you see your doctor, tell him to forget the pills and to just simply make you the doctor and he'll be the patient. Tell him he needs to pay you for *your valuable time*. This dynamic where one human being has to pay another human being for his or her advice is enough in itself to depress the person paying and to make the receiver "feel good." He or she gets paid, gets to give advice, and feels needed. The patient feels lousy and comes out of the meeting poorer for it.

Anyway, in general—if "they" (meaning the multi-billion dollar anti-depressant/mood stabilizer industry) could prove the way they work (show you proof), they would've done so by now and come up with some sort of brain scan that shows your levels before and after a depressive or manic-depressive episode. They say they're "working on it." I say we'll be waiting forever because it just isn't true. It is the human energy transaction first (as the ***root cause*** of "mental illness") and then body chemistry is possibly (probably) altered. You feel "good" or "bad" depending on if you feel like you are "winning" or "losing" in the game of life. Winning or losing human energy that is. I hereby present my expert witnesses for my case:

The Trial of Reality Begins

Here is the Physics (and my very impressive parade of experts):

Me: "I hereby present my case for reality. I call upon Mr. Newton to take the stand, please, and offer his expert testimony."

#1 Sir Isaac Newton

Newton's third law of motion states:

> III. For every action there is an equal and opposite reaction.

"For every action there is an equal and opposite reaction." This law is exemplified by what happens if we step off a boat onto the bank of a lake: as we move in the direction of the shore, the boat tends to move in the opposite direction (leaving us facedown in the water, if we aren't careful!).

Question: What does this have to do with "human energy dynamics?"
Answer: Energy is never lost; it's just transferred around. The theory that connects Newton with human reality is that the nervous system (all human energy systems actually—but for ease of conversation we'll stick with the nervous system) is an energy or action balancing out mechanism. In other words, every second that we pay attention to whom or what, it is a zero sum game. We must also always remember that human attention to a who or a what in Newtonian terms is "action." Therefore, attention also equals energy —"human energy." If all action has an equal and opposite reaction, that means in every interaction someone will walk away feeling worse, better, or exactly even because the nervous system is constantly being conditioned.

Me: "I call upon Mr. Einstein to take the stand, please, and offer his expert testimony."

#2 Albert Einstein

The "special theory of relativity" explains the interchangeability of mass and energy. In his fourth paper, published in September 1905, Einstein discussed a result of the special theory of relativity—that energy and mass are interchangeable. Einstein's paper contains an equation that has become famous: $E = mc^2$. The equation says that a body's energy, E, equals the body's mass, m, times the speed of light, c, squared (multiplied by itself). The speed of light is so high that the conversion of a tiny quantity of mass releases a tremendous amount of energy.

Question: What does this have to do with "human energy dynamics?"
Answer: Einstein's very famous equation backs up Newton's 3rd law of motion which is that *energy is never lost*. It may change form, it may be "locked up" in mass, but it is never lost. As stated in the beginning of this book (in human energy terms),

$E = mc^2$ = E (released energy) = mass (condensed energy) x c^2 (selfishness to exist without mental suffering). Once again the constant is selfishness, because all humans fear, avoid, and attempt to relieve such things as psychological and emotional suffering. And rightly so!

Me: "I call upon the two laws of thermodynamics to offer their expert testimony."

#3 Laws of Thermodynamics

The field of thermodynamics studies the behavior of energy flow in natural systems. From this study, a number of physical laws have been established. The laws of thermodynamics describe some of the fundamental truths of thermodynamics observed in our Universe. Understanding these laws is important to students of human energy dynamics because the processes studied in thermodynamics involve the flow of energy.

First Law of Thermodynamics

The first law of thermodynamics is often called the **law of conservation of energy**. This law suggests that energy can be transferred from one system to another in many forms. However, it cannot be created nor destroyed. Thus, the total amount of energy available in the Universe is constant. Einstein's famous equation (written below) describes the relationship between energy and matter: $E = mc^2$

This law is also consistent with Newton's third law of motion (energy is never lost, just transferred around).

Question: What does this have to do with "human energy dynamics?"
Answer: Once again, energy is never lost, just transferred around.

Second Law of Thermodynamics

Question: Who cares about the second law of thermodynamics?
Answer: Anyone who wonders how the material world of energy and matter works. The second law is ***the biggest, most powerful, most general idea in all of science. This law is the backbone to "human energy dynamics."*** Why the sun will eventually cool down; why iron rusts; why there are hurricanes or any weather at all on earth, what makes things break; why houses get torn apart in tornadoes or explosions; why everything eventually dies.
Question: What *is* the second law of thermodynamics?
Answer: Heat can never pass spontaneously from a colder to a hotter body. As a result of this fact, natural processes that involve energy transfer must have one direction, and all natural processes are irreversible. This law also predicts that the entropy of an isolated system always increases with time. Entropy is the measure of the disorder or randomness of energy and matter in a system. Because of the second law of thermodynamics perfect order in the Universe occurred the instance after the Big Bang when energy and mass and all of the forces of the Universe were unified. In plain English, this ***law states that energy tends to condense before it releases (like an avalanche).***

In short: *"Energy tends to flow from being concentrated or condensed in one place to becoming diffused or dispersed and spread out."*

Question: What does this have to do with "human energy dynamics"?

Answer: As children and young adults we condensed energy/mass through our nervous system conditioning by acquiring such things as credentials and attention. As adults we need to release this energy. ***There is an order to people as to how much energy they had condensed.*** There is an order to all species including humans. The order in humans is a hierarchical structure of condensed energy, released energy, and a multi-faceted hybrid or combination of both types of mass/energy. This is why the "perceived fair exchange of energy" is different for each of us. This is where *entitlement lurks* and this is why "energy leakage/loss disorder" occurs at different times for different people. This is why there are happy poor people living in dilapidated homes and miserable millionaires living in mansions. It's all simply a question of getting a "perceived fair exchange" of our condensed energy/mass. To be simple and frank: We demand credit for who we perceive we are. If we don't get a "perceived fair exchange," our nervous system reacts painfully since bleeding energy or "energy leakage/loss disorder" is very painful. The reason why it's so painful is because our bodies recognize the loss of something so precious, so scarce, and extremely vital to our well-being, peace of mind, and overall survival. The pain we feel is part of natural selection so that we can get our mass/energy back that we feel we deserve because ***it was ours to begin with.*** This is where entitlement comes from—the subconscious feeling that we human beings have a right to get back the condensed energy we held in our nervous systems to begin with via more condensed energy, released energy, or any suitable combination of both.

Physics and Entitlement

"People get and manifest what they perceive they deserve." The truth of the matter is that *entitlement* and deservedness are real, legitimate feelings, and are characteristics of people who perceive themselves as overall high scorers on the multicategorical score-sheet. While it is true they never verbalize it that way, I am here to do it for them.

The second Law of Thermodynamics is so important, so vital to our discussions that it must become crystal clear and I will harp on it now:

An example will illustrate this vital concept: First, imagine a brick resting on a window ledge three stories high. As the brick rests on the ledge, it has potential energy (mgh). If you knock the brick off the ledge the potential energy is converted to kinetic energy as the brick accelerates toward the ground. Then when the brick hits the ground the kinetic energy is converted to light energy (sparks), sound energy (a bang), and chemical energy (the brick breaks).

Now let's merge ***this concept of physics with human beings, and put in human energy terms (the point of the book).*** Let's say you are bred (condensed) with energy (best schools, best looks, best clubs, best breeding, best hotels, best food, most money, most attention, most countries traveled, etc.)—that's the brick sitting on the ledge on the third floor (the higher the stories the more condensed energy/mass you have). Others may have started on an even higher floor (for example—the fourth floor). Think JFK Jr., or Prince William. You must become aware of this fact to understand what is really going on in reality. If you begin to release your mass/condensed energy (the brick starts to fall off the ledge), and set your energy in motion (attention/internal perceptions and physical labor), your brick (you) is now beginning to pay attention and/or perceive people and things. As you begin this process and pay attention and/or perceive people and things, your nervous system will alert you via painful feelings or not if the exchange is a perceived fair one or not. When you exchange with your energy field (aura or vibe) to that of your object you must always remember that energy will not be lost. This is when the brick emits sparks, a bang, a noise and breaks, etc. All the energy that had been condensing inside the brick (you) simply had to go somewhere when it begins to release. In the case of humans, the brick (that's you and I now); we emit moods, feelings, and emotions (instead of the sparks from the brick). In other words, the brick's emotions are its sparks, noise it makes when it hits something, and it's breaking apart. Obviously, the higher the floor we started the more condensed energy we had inside us *to begin with.*

Dating, Projects Not Completed but Being Worked on, and "Potential Energy"

The Brick Again:

"As the brick rests on the ledge, it has *potential* energy (mgh). If you knock the brick off the ledge the potential energy is converted to kinetic energy as the brick accelerates toward the ground. Then when the brick hits the ground the kinetic energy is converted to light energy (sparks), sound energy (a bang), and chemical energy (the brick breaks)."

Once again now: Let's say you are bred (condensed energy/mass) with energy (best schools, best looks, best clubs, most money etc)—that's the brick sitting on the ledge on the third floor (the higher the stories the more condensed energy you have). Others may have started on higher floors etc. When you begin to release your energy and set your energy in motion (attention), your brick (you) will **start to want to date others as you look for human energy in the forms of love, compassion,**

understanding, sex, attention and money. You will also have to work in life to make money and do projects, etc.

Now here is the point: How old are you in this example?

When we are younger we date primarily based on "potential energy." This is because we are a condensed form of energy interacting with other condensed forms of energy. However as we get older, "potential/condensed energy" is no longer as important or valuable as "released energy." This is because we know our lives and our attention are finite and we have less and less tolerance for dating people with "potential/condensed energy." As we get older our entitlement issues surface and energy classes are established. So, our "potential energy" energy class could be very different from our actual or released "energy class." What good are we to another if we just carry around all this "potential energy"? If there is a big age difference in the partners, then we simply have one person's "potential energy" dating someone who has "released energy." Either way, entitlement and "energy class" is behind everything. The point of this teaching is to understand and simplify this complex subject by using a human's age. The age difference creates (by its very nature) different types of energy that are exchanging. There is "potential energy" and "released energy," and of course all nuances in between. On a daily basis we condense and release energy (talking, exercise etc.) Either way, the nervous system recognizes both forms as either a fair current exchange or future fair locked up "potential" exchange or not. This same concept is also true for any project or job you start. If you are starting "low," and the job is "beneath you" currently and you still feel okay, then what you are really exchanging with is the "potential energy" of the job/project. As we get older "potential energy" gets less and less important because people begin to want people who have "released energy," otherwise known as *results*. In the reality where I live, when you are exchanging with a who or a what, you are exchanging with "potential/condensed/mass" energy and "released energy." The nervous system recognizes both intuitively, and can sense the total net effect for its overall well-being, and what the equal and "fair exchange" is. It is a constantly changing multi-faceted hybrid dynamic of various forms of energy.

Question: Do you want a "real world" example?
Answer: I am writing this book mostly because of its "potential energy." As I write—I am not getting any energy in return except for its "potential." As I sit here in isolation, writing, I am in fact "releasing energy"—my attention going into another condensed form—this book. There is no money, love, compassion, etc., coming into me at this moment though I am paying a lot of attention to something (this book). It is the hope (energy) I have for this book that is keeping my attention at this time. I am exchanging with "potential energy" mostly at this time. These writings are a good example of energy condensing from one form to another and the second law of thermodynamics. Another example would be any student at any age going to school to get a degree. So age is just a guide for what I'm talking about. For example, a 65-year-old woman can go to law school (I used age before in the dating example as a guide, that's all), and become a lawyer. While she is in law school (and studying and paying money to be there), if she feels ok doing it, then the so called "sacrifice" is really just her exchanging with "potential or condensed energy." People constantly use words such as "sacrifice," "martyr," or "hero," because they are following law #1 of the laws of human energy dynamics; I will keep hammering this law home over and over again:

Law #1—All human thought and action (including this book) has evolved to be one hundred percent defensive, protective,

selfish, and self-serving so that one can avoid, relieve, reduce, or completely eliminate all forms of suffering via a perceived equal and fair exchange of energy. Overall human energy balance (equilibrium) is what we seek and deserve. Human energy imbalance is the *root cause* of all conceivable forms of human suffering and **all mental illnesses.**
Law #1 explains "self-destructive" and suicidal behavior.
Me: "I call upon Mr. Ivan Pavlov to take the stand, please, and offer his expert testimony."

#4 Ivan Pavlov

Ivan Pavlov was a Russian physiologist who was renowned for his landmark study on conditioning. He conducted this hallmark study during the twentieth century. The interesting thing about this study was the fact that Pavlov was not even studying the effects of conditioning when he launched the study. He was actually studying the physiological effects of eating in the dogs. He began by studying digestion, but Pavlov began to observe that the salivation of the dogs was very curious. He would place meat powder or some other food morsel on the dog's tongue, waiting for the salivation to occur. He began to see that the dogs were salivating as soon as he entered the room, which was before any food was even in sight. Since salivation in any animal is a reflex, Pavlov decided to probe deeper into the conditioning of the dogs. This later became known as classical conditioning. Pavlov's study is also known as Pavlovian conditioning. This study is one of the most used studies in classical conditioning. Conditioning is a type of learning. Basically, what this study proved was that the dogs became conditioned by Pavlov to have expectations. When he entered the room, the dogs expected food; therefore, they began salivating in expectation. After he noticed that the meat powder had this effect, he decided to try a different neutral stimulus. A neutral stimulus is something that normally would not produce any salivation. Pavlov chose to ring a bell since ringing a bell would not normally produce salivation in the dogs. Pavlov began ringing a bell before placing the meat powder or item on the dog's tongue. Each and every time that the bell was rung, meat powder or food was given to the dog. Pavlov repeated these experiments many, many times. Eventually, the bell alone was enough to make the dogs salivate. This proved that a neutral stimulus that elicited no response whatsoever from the dogs before was now causing a response—salivation.

Question: What did this prove with regards to human energy dynamics?

Answer: Pavlov's experiment proved that all animals could be trained or conditioned to expect a consequence on the results of previous experience. For example, a child that is always given a cookie by a particular teacher will begin to expect that cookie every single time that he or she sees the teacher. If the teacher always says the word "yummy" before giving the cookie, the child will become conditioned to expect the cookie after hearing the word.

Pavlov's experiment shows why we are on a "conditioned nervous system" assignment or "mass/energy assignment" while on planet earth. In other words, if we get used to certain things and our nervous system has "expensive" conditioning (say, a very expensive delicious cookie), we then begin to expect certain things in life that equal this level of conditioning. Then we subconsciously and/or consciously feel *entitled* to our expectation and will become depressed, anxious, and demanding when we don't get our perceived fair exchange of energy. *This is because the energy was ours to begin with.* Other people don't understand us because they don't bleed invisible energy. Always remember that energy is never lost, just transferred around.

Me: "I call upon Mr. Darwin to take the stand, please, and offer his expert testimony."

#5 Charles Darwin

Darwin is generally credited with the theory of evolution by natural selection. Natural selection is that the strongest survive and propagate and therefore increase the strength of the species.

Question: How does this relate to human energy dynamics?
Answer: Why does suicide occur? It goes against natural selection. In other words, we humans should simply be able to weed out the thoughts that do not increase our chances of survival, and obviously suicidal thoughts are not helpful to our survival. We should be able to in theory talk ourselves into being in a good mood if we believe in natural selection of thoughts. If natural selection exists in the physical realm, why doesn't psychological and/or emotional Darwinism exist? The answer is when one bumps up against the invisible force of human energy dynamics and experiences an over-abundant energy state (guilt/more than one feels entitled to), an invisible energy bloodbath, "energy leakage/loss" or "energy hemorrhage," the pain is so great that the human's life instinct and will to live is slowly or quickly destroyed. Human energy imbalance syndrome is *very painful* and it comes in all different strengths and degrees. All the human wants to do is to get out of his/her suffering and sees no alternative besides taking his or her own life. This is why many people from old money jumped out of windows and committed suicide when they lost all their money in the stock market crash of 1929. This was a sudden and drastic loss of scarce, finite, ultimately impersonal, impartial neutral human energy—an "energy mhemorrhage" so to speak.

Me: "Lastly, I call upon Mr. Hawking to take the stand, please, and offer his expert testimony."

#6 Stephen Hawking

On January 23, 2003 Hawking made a speech about the ultimate theory of the universe:

In a live broadcast from England to several classrooms at MIT, physicist Stephen Hawking described scientists' search for a complete theory of the universe, **ultimately concluding that "maybe [such a theory] isn't possible."**

"Some people will be very [disappointed] if there is not an ultimate theory," Hawking said. "I belong to that camp, but I have changed my mind." We will "always have the challenge of new discovery. Without it, we will stagnate. Long may the search continue?" Hawking essentially gave a brief history of particle physics, focusing on the key scientists and theories in the field from Aristotle to Stephen Weinberg (a Nobel laureate born in 1933).

The Maxwell and Dirac equations, for example, "govern most of physics and all of chemistry and biology," Hawking said. "So in principle we should be able to predict human behavior, though I can't say I've had much success myself," he said to chuckles from the audience.

Question: How does this relate to human energy dynamics?

Answer: Read what Mr. Hawking said again. Number one, he said, "We will always have the challenge of a new discovery. Without it, we will stagnate. Long may the search continue," and number two, "So in principle, we should be able to predict human behavior." So what he is saying is that a book like this should in fact be possible. This book has the two things he spoke about: (1) *challenging new discoveries* and (2) *theories for predicting human behavior.*

Doorway Eighteen of reality

Teaching: Human Energy is finite

The Universe/Creator/Whatever may be finite, infinite and/or both (Stephen Hawking still isn't even sure); human beings are finite in this particular incarnation. Not only that we are hardwired to fear death, dying, and especially suffering. *Energy leakage/loss disorder creates suffering and so does over-abundant energy condition;* It's that simple. If one cannot figure out how to recoup their energy loss or get rid of the over-abundance they are holding (guilt), they will either commit suicide or have a breakdown that will literally force the human energy imbalance issue. The breakdown *(as is all behavior)* is a defense mechanism so that the person can get human attention (energy) equilibrium and/or make amends for the terrible guilt they are holding. If the breakdown was caused by guilt, then this person will not want to cause others more pain; rather will hope to explain their troubles to people in the psych hospital which can relieve them of their guilt (getting too much human energy—more than one feels entitled to). This person was unable to say certain things to certain people while on "the outside" and needed to have a breakdown to make up for the guilt he or she held inside.

Since we humans in this form are finite and this is indisputable and we are made up of energy (we are not plugged into an outlet, for example, we just go), we therefore have finite human energy. It's the simple math equation if a = b and b = c therefore a = c. If humans are finite = a, and humans are energy = b, therefore humans equal finite energy (a = c). This is what we compete for every second of our lives. The infinite energy of the universe/God (if it is infinite) is there for us to "tap into" when we pay attention to it. Infinite internal perceptions cannot occur because planet earth is a finite place. Clashing *entitlement for safety* will always occur when two or more people feel *entitled* to the same exact thing. Everyone cannot be a King or Queen as the Universe will check and balance your nervous system and conditions it to take its rightful place in the hierarchy. The whole trick in life is learning to accept where you fit in and not over-step or under-step where you belong in the hierarchy. *Be content and accept where you fit in.* This takes time. At a certain age—you will make peace with where you fit in. If you don't—you may end up committing suicide or get very sick physically. Make awareness your best defense.

Back to our discussions:

Condensed energy (internal perceptions) cannot talk to us, clothe us, feed us, shelter us, or give us money. These things take up the human energy we compete for. The Universe/God/Whatever may or may not be infinite, and even if it were infinite it is still in competition for our energy like everything else. In other words, *our attention* is what external energy forms compete for. God and the Universe must compete for it like everything else and must in effect, "get in line." Our internal perceptions are our internal energy while all other forms of energy are external forms of energy. Once again, it's worth repeating: God must get in line behind people, making money, movies, books, and television shows and compete for our limited finite attention spans (like everyone and everything else.)

Before the "Big Bang," I do not know how the Universe or God was created nor do I care. All I care about is why there is so much stress and conflict on this planet, and why guilt, depression, anxiety, and mental illness occur at all. My answer and theory is now clear: All human behavior is driven by the pursuit of the human energy I speak of, and the amount one needs to survive comfortably is different and unique for each of us (entitlement issues).

The intensity of the emotions is in proportion to the perceived gain or loss of energy in every exchange. In other words, the amount you perceived gained or lost will be the degree and strength of your feelings. Here's a little twist:

If you gain more energy than you feel entitled to, you will feel guilty and this much is clear. This is hard to do actually because abundance is such a good defense (in case of a rainy day etc.). So in order to feel really guilty, one has to feel *overabundant* with regards to energy. Once over-abundance occurs, the human will feel guilt and so he or she won't implode—he or she will release his energy to charities or "help other people" etc. This is the selfish need of a human being to remove guilt.

Entitlement is secretly lurking behind everything.

Real World Example:

You buy a hot dog for $2.00. You give the seller a $10 bill, but he mistakes it for a $20 and gives you back change of $18 instead of $8. What do you do?

Answer # 1: If you feel *entitled* to the extra $10, you keep it. You will feel "lucky" and that you deserved a break. This is now a perceived fair exchange of energy.
Answer # 2: If you don't feel *entitled* to the extra $10, you will feel guilty (more than a fair exchange of energy) and give the money back.

Once again, the energy exchange is causing the emotion *not* "chemical imbalances" or "faulty brain chemistry". **Since energy is so scarce and finite, it is the most precious resource on planet earth. Guard equilibrium with your life.**

Doorways Nineteen through Twenty-One

Teaching: Right Now

We are entering the final few sections now. Take a moment and understand the moment you are now in. You are reading a book about what reality means to a fellow human being on planet earth. Three doorways dedicated to staying in the moment and to the realization that what you are now reading is extremely powerful. Accept selfishness and the competitive nature for human energy as a reality. It's a certain way of looking at reality that's all.

SECTION FOUR

A Matter Of Reality

Doorway Twenty-Two of reality

Teaching: Thinking Poolside

Once again I am seated at a high-energy place. Today I am at the Hotel Palacio in Estoril, Portugal (I was born right near here on July 23, 1971). I've been told this hotel is the "playground of royalty;" and that it is ranked as one of the world's most luxurious hotels. The hotel shines of old world charm as its lobby is decorated in such a way that shows its reverence to marble. Anyway, here I am, poolside on a beautiful hot, clear (not a cloud in the sky) September day. This is day number nine for me here and I've of course done nothing (except tan, play golf and tennis), and ponder the true nature of reality. What else is new? As I sit here paying attention to my writings, I feel relaxed and productive. I am finally beginning to release my condensed energy. I begin to wonder what doctors will think of this text. I smirk because it is obvious to me that they have tunnel vision in the specialty that they know about. This is human nature—to specialize and have an area of expertise. I, on the other hand, specialize in nothing on the one hand, but also everything on the other. You see, it is clear to me that energy is bred into your nervous system and that subconsciously and perhaps consciously, your nervous system demands its perceived fair exchange of energy (all human energy systems that get conditioned as we go through life). Basically, the nervous system feels *entitled* to this and will not stop until it gets this perceived fair exchange. Everything we do in life is programmed into us in a COST-BENEFIT analysis. The cost is basically money and/or the psychological cost (any type of mental or physical suffering that leads to suffering) of doing something and/or anything. It (conditioned human energy systems) simply cannot relax any other way. The *entitlement* comes from how one perceives its weighted summation of rankings in the "multi-categorical score chart." This comes from how we were raised and how society received us. Many women, for example, feel **entitled** to people's attention and things by virtue of their perceived sexual attractiveness. We all know how important rankings are to human experience.

When one cannot figure out how to get this perceived fair exchange, a breakdown will occur which will force the issue (attention and/or money). I hope doctors question their patients about their feelings of **entitlement** and perceptions of where they fit in on each category and then work with their clients from there. In each category there is a truth. Some people are more attractive, have better credentials, better breeding and lineage, and are simply more intelligent, etc. Basically, overall, people are ranked by their cumulative score in all the categories and become who they are—a blend of everything.

What their perceived score is determines their level of entitlement for the marketplace of human energy. The feeling of entitlement is present at birth. As humans we take up space and are made of energy. By our births, we are entitled to energy. How much energy we are entitled to is the magic question. The magic answer is—it is determined by our entitlement feelings (multi-categorical score sheet overall score). Human energy equals love, compassion, understanding, hope, money, attention, etc.

The sun is straight over me now. This Portuguese sun is very hot! I think it's time for lunch. It must be close to 2:00 P.M. now. I love this dry heat actually. It reminds me of Arizona. The breeze makes this place so pleasant, and my father tells me how lucky I am to be here. Meanwhile, I sit here writing this to figure out and share the true nature of reality with the world one day. The pool in front of me is also big and beautiful. I think I'll go for a swim and bring my attention to the Palacio's pool. At this exact moment, swimming would be a perceived fair exchange of my energy. Energy is not particularly a tricky concept, really. Anything that can turn into money or anything that money can buy is basically energy (there are many forms, but money is quantifiable). Physical appearance (the better looking you think you are is the more energy you have) is energy because people will pay money (prostitution) for sex, and attention is energy because people pay people to pay attention to them (therapy).

So this energy is bred into us (via our nervous systems)—physical appearance, where and the style in which we grew up, where we went to school, credentials, attention, love, compassion, friendship, hope is all part of the condensed energy that we were brought up with (conditioned our nervous system along the way). Then as adults, we interact subconsciously with our "multi-categorical score sheet" of how we perceive people, things, and ourselves. You see, one of the *main discoveries* of these theories (yes there are many) is that there are *ENERGY CLASSES* of people and only like energy classes can exchange fairly (in a hypothetical social vacuum). Every second of your life is business. The business of energy competition.

Doorway Twenty-Three of reality

Teaching: Discussion of Energy Class

Energy class is your perception of your ranking in the hierarchy of people. I'm sorry to say that this philosophy—the philosophy of human energy dynamics—most definitely sees a ranking in all categories and therefore a ranking to all people. The good news is you can gain or lose energy in life and therefore change energy classes.

Let's say we have five energy classes: A, B, C, D and E. An A person would perceive his rankings in the multi-categorical score sheet of energy to be, in summation, very high. He/she would be a very good looking male/female from a high socioeconomic background many generations deep and perceive himself as superior in almost every category. He/she was bred with a lot of energy (money, breeding, hope, etc.). Remember perception is reality and one must perceive himself/herself to be superior as a mix to be at the top of the pyramid of energy class. Think JFK, Jr., or Prince William and you've got the idea.

Micro-Energy

Energy can be made and lost every single second of every single day. Example, someone can find money on the street; someone takes good care of themselves before a party and feels more attractive for an evening out; someone has a coincidental encounter with a love interest. On a micro-level it's a moment-to-moment thing. Energy condenses and releases each day.

Macro-Energy

In general, a peasant who wins the lottery will only have advanced in one category—please note. The peasant will have wealth but not all the other categories. The children of the newly enriched peasant will not do well in the "lineage" category and will not have made great gains in all the categories in general. However, if the money stays in the family for another two to five generations, progress can be made once the children and grandchildren go to better and better schools and get better and better "breeding," etc. It can also be lost the same way. A very wealthy family could lose all their money in a stock market crash or lose their business altogether suddenly. Other examples, a person can simply lose their looks and/or their job. This is energy leakage.

In a Theoretical Sex Vacuum

Sex is a matter of personal pride. Who you have intimate relations with is directly connected to your brain via your perceptions/thoughts about yourself and that other person. In effect it is one multi-categorical score sheet, going to bed with another. If the exchange is a perceived fair one, love can blossom. Sex is a form of human energy.

Question: What is love?

Doorway Twenty-Four of reality

Teaching: More Details of the Score Chart

Category 1: Determining Social Class: Socioeconomic Status (SES)

Socioeconomic status (SES) calls attention the complex nature of social class.

There are objective measures of social class. Henslin (1999:253) suggests that researchers can assign people to various social classes based objective criteria involving wealth, power, and prestige. Some objective indicators can include occupation, educational level, number of dependents, type of residence, infant mortality, and life expectancy rates. There are also subjective measures. Typically, determining class from a subjective point of view involves asking someone how they perceive their class position.

Finally, class can be determined using the reputation method (Henslin 1999:253). People identify an individual's social class based on their expert knowledge of their individual's circumstances. The reputation method is limited to smaller communities, where people are familiar with one another's reputation. People at each class level see class differently. They, therefore, carry around different personal pictures of society's classes. People see finer divisions at their own class level, but tend to lump together people who occupy other class levels. For example, people at the top see several divisions of people at the top while they see one large monolithic group of people at the bottom. On the other hand, people at the bottom see several distinctions of poor people, but only one group at the top—the rich (Henslin 1999:253).

Weber offers a multidimensional class model that incorporates three distinct entities: Economic status (wealth), political status (power), and social status (prestige).

A. Wealth

Wealth consists of assets and income.

Robertson (1989:180) contends that while the US is philosophically indebted to the notion that "all men are created equal," the US is, in fact, a very stratified society. The US has the most inegalitarian class structures in the industrialized world (Long 1993).

For the first century of nationhood in the US, a caste system was in place in the form of racial slavery. Many of the familiar characteristics associated with the Indian caste system were in effect. Included in America's caste system were endogamy and notions of ritual pollution. Blacks were not allowed in the same restaurants, bathrooms, and buses as whites. Women also can be seen as occupying secondary position in a caste system. Despite the professed commitment to human rights, the US today contains 600,000 millionaires and 32 million people below the poverty line.

1. Assets

Wolff (Skolnick and Currie 1997:99) describes assets as consisting of all forms of "financial wealth such as bank accounts, stocks, bonds, life insurance savings, mutual fund shares and unincorporated business; consumer durables like cares and major appliances; and the value of pension rights." Wolff (1997:99) continues to say that from these sources, one should subtract liabilities such as "consumer debt, mortgage balances, and other outstanding debt." The upper classes control a much greater percentage of valuable assets than income. Robertson (1989:180) points out that in 1973 the bottom fifth of Americans controlled only 0.2 percent of all assets while the top fifth controlled 76 percent of all assets. Further, the assets controlled by the poor tend to depreciate (household items) over time while those of the rich tend to appreciate (real estate and stocks).

2. Income

Appelbaum & Chambliss (1997:134) defines income as "the amount of money a person or household earns in a given period of time (usually a year)." The gap between rich and poor is also very unequal and it is increasing.

B. Power

Power is the ability to see that one's will is acted upon. Powerful people are able to mobilize resources to achieve their goals despite resistance from others. Henslin (1999) argues that it is an inevitable part of everyday life. Like wealth, power is concentrated in the hands of a few. Robertson (1989:182) makes an interesting observation with regards to minorities gaining more political power. He argues that just as Blacks, Hispanics, and women are beginning to vote in their respective interests; power is flowing away from public institutions and into the hands of giant bureaucracies and influential private interest groups. Voters, after all, have only one of several possible means of influencing decision makers, i.e., their vote.

C. Prestige

Prestige refers to the power to impress or influence. It differs from power in that it is based less on political position. Prestige correlates with charisma. A prestigious person has a reputation based on brilliance, achievements, or on character.

Robertson (1989:182) contends that there is much less stratification in terms of prestige in the United States than there is in terms of wealth and power. He suggests that while prestige ranking is obvious, Americans treat each other remarkably well when compared to other countries.

Prestige Ratings of Occupations in the United States
These are prestige ratings of 1 to 100 that average Americans gave to various occupations.

Rank	Occupation	Score
1	Physician	82
2	College Professor	78
3	Judge	77
4	Lawyer	76
5	Physicist	74
6	Dentist	74
95	Waiter	20
96	Farm Laborer	18
97	Maid/Servant	18
98	Garbage Collector	17
99	Janitor	17
100	Shoe Shiner	9

Source: Robertson, 1989:174

1. Maintaining Stratification

The United States has great inequality (See L.I.S. Chart). How is it possible that such an unequal system can exist? Always, the majority is denied the wealth of a few. Revolutions, however, are rare compared to all political activity. Two explanations seem to explain why revolutions are so rare. On one hand, the dominant class controls resources. On the other hand, there is widespread belief that the rule of the upper class is legitimate. Marx notes that social institutions tend to reflect the will of the dominant class. This does not mean that the ruling class actually plots to control institutions.

2. Social Networks

The government does not conspire to control all wealth. The rich act in their common interests by simply knowing each other and by sharing a common agenda.

3. Legitimacy

Many, even the poor, see the power of the rich as legitimate (Weber 1968). The masses view the given political economy as valid and justified.

4. Ideology

An ideology is a set of beliefs, which explain, or justify some actual or potential social arrangement (Robertson 1989:176). An ideology confers legitimacy on a social system. Marx argued that legitimizing the social stratification pattern was an important function for ideology.

    A.   False Consciousness
        Robertson's (1989:176) definition is "a subjective understanding that does not correspond with the objective facts of one's situation." The poor do not realize that their miseries are a shared phenomenon that results from their oppressed status. Instead of blaming the system they blame their circumstances on fate, an act of god, luck, or other factors beyond their control.

    B.   Class Consciousness
        Class-consciousness refers to "an objective awareness of the lower stratum's common plights and interests as an oppressed group." At this point they begin to question

the legitimacy of the system. They begin to build their own ideology, which justifies and supports their class interests and consequently seems revolutionary to the dominant stratum.

5. Portraits of the Classes

The following material is taken from Charon (1986). The percentages are rough estimates.

A. Upper Class (1 percent of total population)
   The upper class consists of relatively few individuals and families (a small executive club) with great wealth and great power in the economy. Generally, the upper class inherit their wealth. It comes in the form of property and other assets. While this group does not have to work, they often serve on the boards of directors of major corporations. From this vantage point, the upper class occupies a position from which they can have great impact on the course of world history. The upper class has a certain life style in which individuals are careful to socialize only with the "right crowd."

B. Upper Middle Class (10 Percent)
   The upper middle class consists of "successful business people, executives, professionals, and high ranking civil and military officials." Ownership of business as well as prestigious occupations brings wealth to these individuals. Most have high levels of education. The wealth of this class comes from investment and savings. Unlike in the upper class, they inherit little of their wealth. This group is very active politically and culturally.

C. Middle Class (30 percent)
   The lower middle class also consists of professionals, semi-professionals and small business people. People who

make up the middle class are less affluent and occupy fewer prestigious positions than the upper middle class. The middle class includes nurses, teachers, police officers, and social workers. The middle class includes most of the white-collar work force and others who earn "respectable" livings. Jobs for this group are generally secure. The middle class is well educated. They also have great political impact. It was this group after all, who got us out of Vietnam and who led the California tax rebellion.

D. Working Class (40 percent)

The working class consists of skilled and unskilled workers (blue collar workers), factory workers, farm hands, sales personnel, and low-level clerical workers. Usually these positions do not require college. Although many in this class belong to unions, it is not, as a rule, an effective political force. Jobs performed by this group are routine, mechanized, and closely supervised. These jobs are less secure than jobs performed by people in the middle class.

The nature of work performed by the working class has changed. On one hand the backbreaking work that used to characterize the working class has evolved into less physically demanding work. Regardless, work performed at this level is none-the-less still tedious. It is also boring. The working class is less secure now than in the past. As corporation shift their operations offshore, jobs traditionally done by this group are now performed by Third-Worlders.

E. Lower Class (20 percent)

The lower class consists of the poor. The lower class experiences high rates of unemployment and dependency on government, employers, the state of the economy, and landlords. People from the lower class are not likely to succeed in the educational system. They experience prejudice from the legal system. This class seldom exerts itself politically.

F. The Under Class (1 percent)

See William Julius Wilson (1980, 1987)

6. Consequences of Class Position/Dating and Marriage

Children tend to seek out those who act, speak, and have the same cultural values as themselves. The upper class also arranges social events such that upper class children meet only upper class children.

A. Socialization

Class also shapes values and norms and these norms and values in turn determine how people act in social settings like school and occupation. Middle-class children grow up valuing independence more than working-class people while working-class people prefer conformity.

B. Health

In general, the higher the social class, the greater the life expectancy. The poor are subject to more infant deaths and disease than the upper classes. Rates of mental illness also go up as social class goes down and the poor are less likely to receive treatment. The higher level of stress is one explanation for higher rates of mental illness.

C. Formal Education

Class correlates with education in a number of ways. Since education is community based, class determines the quality of teachers and curriculum. Teachers have middle class backgrounds and, therefore, work better with students "like themselves." The importance of education receives greater emphasis in upper classes; therefore, children of the upper classes are more likely to attend college.

Class Level	% that attends college
Upper Class	88%
Lower Middle	64%
Upper Working	40%
Lower Working	15%

It should be noted that since there is an order to the universe, it should be noted that earth is just part of the universe. Humans are the most superior life form on planet earth. It is therefore easily understood that in the cosmic pecking order or "universal food chain" there may be superior life forms to humans.

As you can see, I went into detail on one category—socioeconomic class. This category is, in my opinion, a very powerful one for energy because so many energy fields (money flows) go into it. I personally would weigh this category very strongly. However just being from a high socioeconomic class does not give you superior energy. You may be from the highest socioeconomic class but extremely ugly and nerdy at the same time. This is why I insist energy comes from the overall score on the multi-categorical score chart and not just one, two, three or even ten categories.

Many More Categories In Detail Now

Sexuality

Assumption: All prostitutes are in a "sex vacuum." This means all other variables such as current money needs are equal.

In the case of prostitution, energy is exchanged (money) to make the exchange a perceived fair one. Your price is your worth. The customer: how you feel about yourself afterward will condition you as to whether or not you will make that same exchange or not in the future. *It's not just the market* that determines the price: *it's the market PLUS entitlement feelings.*

Where from/live now category

New York Superior?

Note: This is what Einstein called a "frame of reference."

As people we are products of our environments. Is New York City superior? Many people perceive that it is. For the past century,

New York City, while imperfect, has been the center of civilization in the modern world. Many agree that the reason why September 11, 2001 mostly happened in Manhattan, New York City was because no place other than New York would have had such an impact on the demands of the world's attention. New York is a global phenomenon. It is the world's center, the cultural and spiritual melting pot, and the biggest city in the world's most powerful nation. New York is perceived to be one of the world's most dynamic cities, if not clearly perceived as the world's most superior city for many reasons. Its magnetism is second to none as people from all over the world flock here to fulfill their karmic destinies. New York offers infinite opportunities for personal expansion and spiritual growth. New York's energy is apparent to anyone who has ever lived or spent considerable time here. New York remains a leader in finance, arts, culture, and intellectual pursuits. It is the perception of many people on this planet that New York City is the center and the unofficial capital of planet earth for the past 100 years. This is why the real estate values (dollar per square foot) for residential and commercial space is among the highest in the world (if not the highest). Hong Kong and London are up there too.

As New Yorkers we are privileged to live in one of the greatest cities on the planet. A diverse melting pot, rich with talents in the arts, business, fashion and media, "the city" is a treasure chest. As the *financial capital, the fashion center, the advertising capital, and the cultural repository* for our great nation, New York City sets the pace for modern society. Not to mention the *Yankees. No place is this influence more apparent than in the images reflected in popular culture. The propensity of images broadcast from of images broadcast from Hollywood and Madison Avenue reflect values and struggles that are personified by New York City. Not only is New York City a magnifying glass for issues relevant to American society (the world's most powerful nation), challenges now face us on the world stage as we became the focus of a terrible terrorist attack to the "heart and soul" of the United States. Did I mention the United Nations is here also? One could argue that Manhattan is the capital of New York and that the Upper East Side is the capital of Manhattan. Once again, it's all perception. One could easily think London, Jerusalem, Mecca, Baghdad, etc., was the center of the world in their perception.

*Let's talk about sports:

We all know and can admit how much attention (human energy) is given to sports.

When New Yorkers think about jobs in sports, the usually focus on the 25 players on the Yankees or Mets, the 12 on the Knicks or Nets and the 53 on the Jets and Giants. Don't forget hockey with the Rangers, Islanders and Devils. But sports jobs in New York go well beyond the Derek Jeters and Jason Kidds because the city is BY FAR the nation's number one sports metropolis. New York has more than 5,000 year round sports related jobs—from $20,000 a year jobs to the likes of George Steinbrenner. And this doesn't include all the part-time vendors, ticket-takers, and security guards, etc., for game time. The New York metro area not only has more sports teams than any other American city, but it is also the home of league offices, sports agents, players' labor unions, law firms, public relations firms, and advertising agencies that do sports business. New York is clearly the worldwide epicenter for sports business activity.

Here is just a sample of more things the New York City metro area offers. There are many more such as minor league baseball in Staten Island and Brooklyn, amusement parks, and embassies/consulates etc.

Entertainment	Cultural Societies	Museums	Aquarium, Gardens & Zoos
USTA Tennis Center	Asia Society	American craft Museum	Brooklyn Botanic Garden
Meadowlands – Giants Stadium, Continental Arena, Racetrack	Austrian Institute	American Folk Art Museum	Central Park Wildlife Center

Enlightenment Through Entitlement | 197

Nassau Coliseum	Caribbean Cultural Center	American Museum of Natural History	Tisch Children's Zoo
Madison Square Garden	China Institute Gallery	Children's Museum of Manhattan	The Conservatory Garden
Radio City Music Hall	Chinese Information & Cultural Center	The Cloisters	Queens Botanical Garden
City Center	Ellis Island	Cooper-Hewitt, National Design Museum	Staten Island Botanical Garden
Lincoln Center	French Institute	Guggenheim Museum	Prospect Park Zoo
Broadway, Off Broadway, and Off-off Broadway Shows	Goethe House New York German	Intrepid Sea-Air Space Museum	Queens Zoo
Carnegie Hall	Irish Arts Center	The Jewish Museum	Staten Island Zoo
Yankee Stadium	Jewish Museum	Madame Tussaud's Wax Museum	Bronx Zoo
Shea Stadium	Museum del Barrio	Metropolitan Museum of Art	New York Aquarium
	Museum for African Art	Museum of African Art	New York Botanical Garden
	Polish Institute of Art & Sciences	Museum of the City of New York	

	Shomburg Center for Research in Black Culture	Museum of Jewish Heritage	
	Spanish Institute	Museum of Modern Art	
	Tibetan Museum, Museum of Tibetan Art	Museum of Television and Radio	
	Ukrainian Museum	National Academy of Design	
	Yeshiva University Museum	New York Historical Society	
	Hispanic Society of America	Smithsonian National Museum of the American Indian	
	Museum of Jewish Heritage	South Street Seaport Museum	
	Japan Society	Statue of Liberty Museum	
	Smithsonian National Museum of American Indian	Whitney Museum of American Art	

New York has a deep guarded port and access to fresh water and inland water routes (Hudson River). New York is not a marsh like New Orleans (which has access to Mississippi), but rather it has a lot of bedrock to build on.

Where a person is from/lives is only one category, but there's little doubt it definitely helps define how a person views the world and reality.

Highest household income by town in USA
Income Source: CNNfn 2002

Potomac, Md.	$112,452
Westport, Conn.	110,413
Highland Park, Ill.	97,317
Bloomfield Township, Mich.	97,224
Livingston, N.J.	92,578
Wellesley, Mass.	92,391
McLean, Va.	92,306
Trumbull, Conn.	91,550
Leawood, Kan.	90,906
Rancho Palos Verdes, Calif.	90,280
Olney, Md.	90,223
Bethesda, Md.	89,414
Plainview, N.Y.	89,127
Saratoga, Calif.	88,957
New City, N.Y.	88,417
Oceanside, N.Y.	86,995
Dix Hills, N.Y.	86,916
West Bloomfield Township, Mich.	86,250
Westfield, N.J.	86,221
Paramus, N.J.	86,077
Burke, Va.	85,894
Levittown, N.Y.	85,671
Los Altos, Calif.	85,587
West Springfield, Va.	85,040
Oakton, Va.	84,747

Education/Credentials

2003 Undergrad Liberal Arts Colleges US News & World Report

1.	Amherst College (MA)
2.	Swarthmore College (PA)
	Williams College (MA)
4.	Wellesley College (MA)
5.	Carleton College (MN)
	Pomona College (CA)
7.	Bowdoin College (ME)
	Middlebury College (VT)
9.	Davidson College (NC)
10.	Haverford College (PA)
11.	Wesleyan University (CT)
12.	Grinnell College (IA)
13.	Claremont McKenna College (CA)
	Smith College (MA)
15.	Harvey Mudd College (CA)
	Vassar College (NY)
	Washington and Lee University (VA)
18.	Colby College (ME)
	Colgate University (NY)
	Hamilton College (NY)
21.	Bryn Mawr College (PA)
22.	Bates College (ME)
23.	Mount Holyoke College (MA)
	Oberlin College (OH)
25.	Trinity College (CT)

* denotes a public school.

Undergrad National Universities 2003 Rankings

1.	Princeton University (NJ)
2.	Harvard University (MA)
	Yale University (CT)
4.	California Institute of Technology
	Duke University (NC)
	Massachusetts Inst. of Technology
	Stanford University (CA)
	University of Pennsylvania
9.	Dartmouth College (NH)
10.	Columbia University (NY)
	Northwestern University (IL)
12.	University of Chicago
	Washington University in St. Louis
14.	Cornell University (NY)
15.	Johns Hopkins University (MD)
	Rice University (TX)
17.	Brown University (RI)
18.	Emory University (GA)
	University of Notre Dame (IN)
20.	University of California - Berkeley *
21.	Carnegie Mellon University (PA)
	Vanderbilt University (TN)
23.	University of Virginia *
24.	Georgetown University (DC)
25.	Univ. of California - Los Angeles *

* denotes a public school.

Law School Rankings: 2003 US News & World Report

1.	Yale University (CT)
2.	Stanford University (CA)
3.	Harvard University (MA)
4.	Columbia University (NY)
5.	New York University
6.	University of Chicago
7.	University of Michigan–Ann Arbor
	University of Pennsylvania
9.	University of Virginia
10.	Cornell University (NY)
	University of California–Berkeley
12.	Duke University (NC)
	Northwestern University (IL)
14.	Georgetown University (DC)
15.	University of Texas–Austin
16.	University of California–Los Angeles
17.	Vanderbilt University (TN)
18.	University of Southern California
19.	University of Minnesota–Twin Cities
	Washington and Lee University (VA)
21.	University of Iowa
22.	Boston College
	George Washington University (DC)
	University of Notre Dame (IN)
25.	University of Illinois–Urbana-Champaign

* denotes a public school.

Business School Rankings

Rank	Wall Street Journal (2002)	Business Week	USNWR (-2002)	Forbes National Programs (2002)	Business Education Commission
1	Dartmouth (Tuck)	U Penn (Wharton)	Stanford	Harvard	Harvard
2	Michigan	Northwestern (Kellogg)	Harvard	Pennsylvania (Wharton)	Stanford
3	Carnegie Mellon	Harvard	Northwestern (Kellogg)	Columbia	U Penn (Wharton)
4	Northwestern (Kellogg)	MIT (Sloan)	U Penn (Wharton)	Dartmouth (Tuck)	Chicago
5	U Penn (Wharton)	Duke (Fuqua)	MIT (Sloan)	Chicago	Northwestern (Kellogg)
6	Chicago	Michigan	Columbia	Yale	MIT (Sloan)
7	Texas—Austin (McCombs)	Columbia	UC Berkeley (Haas)	Cornell (Johnson)	Columbia
8	Yale	Cornell (Johnson)	Duke (Fuqua)	MIT (Sloan)	Michigan
9	Harvard	Virginia (Darden)	Chicago	Northwestern (Kellogg)	Dartmouth (Tuck)
10	Columbia	Chicago	Michigan	Stanford	Virginia (Darden)

Here are some rankings of different things in society Worth:

Rank	Name	Worth ($mil)	Age	Marital Status	Residence	Source
1	Gates, William H. III	54,000	45	married	Seattle, WA	Microsoft
2	Buffett, Warren Edward	33,200	71	married	Omaha, NE	investments
3	Allen, Paul Gardner	28,200	48	single	Mercer Island, WA	Microsoft
4	Ellison, Lawrence Joseph	21,900	57	divorced	Atherton, CA	Oracle
5	Walton, Alice L.	17,500	52	divorced	Fort Worth, TX	Wal-Mart
5	Walton, Helen R.	17,500	82	widowed	Bentonville, AR	Wal-Mart
5	Walton, Jim C.	17,500	53	married	Bentonville, AR	Wal-Mart
5	Walton, John T.	17,500	55	married	Durango, CO	Wal-Mart
5	Walton, S. Robson	17,500	57	divorced	Bentonville, AR	Wal-Mart
10	Ballmer, Steven Anthony	15,100	45	married	Redmond, WA	Microsoft
11	Anthony, Barbara Cox	11,300	78	married	Honolulu, HI	Cox Enterprises
11	Chambers, Anne Cox	11,300	81	divorced	Atlanta, GA	Cox Enterprises
13	Kluge, John Werner	10,600	87	married	Charlottesville, VA	Metromedia
14	Redstone, Sumner M.	10,100	78	married	Newton Centre, MA	Viacom
15	Dell, Michael	9,800	36	married	Austin, TX	Dell
16	Anschutz, Philip F.	9,600	61	married	Denver, CO	Qwest Communications
17	Johnson, Abigail	9,100	39	married	Boston, MA	Fidelity
18	Mars, Forrest Edward Jr.	9,000	70	married	McLean, VA	Candy
18	Mars, Jacqueline Badger	9,000	62	divorced	Bedminster, NJ	Candy
18	Mars, John Franklyn	9,000	65	married	Arlington, VA	Candy
21	Murdoch, Keith Rupert	7,500	70	married	New York, NY	publishing
22	Ergen, Charles	7,100	48	married	Denver, CO	satellite TV
23	Soros, George	6,900	71	married	Bedford, NY	money manager
24	Bronfman, Edgar M. Sr.	6,800	72	married	New York, NY	liquor
25	Turner, Robert E. (Ted)	6,200	62	divorced	Atlanta, GA	Turner Broadcasting

Source CnnFn Feb 2003

Most expensive home (real estate) list
Here's a sample (50 top towns) from the Directory of Wealth

RANK	TOWN	POPULATION	MEDIAN PRICE
1.	Aspen, CO	5,049	$1,512,500
2.	Jupiter Island, FL	601	1,222,500
3.	Rolling Hills, CA	1,748	1,165,000
4.	Atherton, CA	7,500	1,150,000
5.	Matinecock, NY (LI)	880	1,070,000
6.	Hillsborough, CA	10,589	1,023,000
7.	Belvedere, CA	2,071	986,000
8.	Rancho Santa Fe, CA	12,300	963,000
9.	Los Altos Hills, CA	7,900	960,000
10.	Snowmass Village, CO	1,449	960,000
11.	Purchase, NY	4,205	950,000
12.	Sands Point, NY	2,477	950,000
13.	Saddle River, NJ	3,136	941,500
14.	North Hills, NY (LI)	3,748	895,000
15.	Old Brookville, NY (LI)	1,914	845,000
16.	Old Westbury, NY (LI)	4,204	810,000
17.	Hidden Hills, CA	1,879	790,000
18.	Portola Valley, CA	4,400	787,250
19.	Monte Sereno, CA	3,311	775,000
20.	Ross, CA	1,894	767,400
21.	Brookville, NY (LI) Upper	3,748	765,000
22.	Brookville, NY (LI)	1,560	765,000
23.	Alpine, NJ	1,849	755,000
24.	Beverly Hills, CA	34,116	750,000
25.	Woodside, CA	5,087	7,742,500
26.	Kenilworth, IL	2,291	740,000
27.	Green Village, NJ	892	736,000
28.	Montecito, CA	10,000	731,000
29.	Bannockburn, IL	1,595	725,000
30.	Hunting Valley, OH	824	712,500
31.	Gulf Stream, FL	789	710,000
32.	Oyster Bay Cove, NY (LI)	2,240	700,000
33.	Bloomfield Hills, MI	4,587	695,000
34.	Muttontown, NY (LI)	3,107	680,000
35.	Palm Beach, FL	9,894	675,000

36.	Diablo, CA	1,158	672,500
37.	Saratoga, CA	27,527	659,500
38.	Kentfield, CA	6,296	655,000
39.	Mill Neck, NY (LI)	985	655,000
40.	Greenwich, CT	36,504	651,000
41.	Palos Verdes Estates, CA	12,847	650,000
42.	Marina del Rey, CA	7,431	645,000
43.	Bronxville, NY	5,992	640,000
44.	New Canaan, CT	17,656	637,500
45.	Kings Point, NY (LI)	4,821	635,000
46.	New Vernon, NJ	722	632,500
47.	Los Altos, CA	27,988	625,000
48.	Wailea, HI	3,798	625,000
49.	Laurel Hollow, NY (LI)	1,784	624,700
50.	Lattingtown, NY (LI)	1,892	610,000

Abstract of Worth Magazine Article

The point is to realize and understand that everything has a ranking. Why shouldn't people be ranked (people are ranked by cross-referencing all categories). Some people are good looking, well educated and rich etc. The answer is they should be. The ranking is a "human energy ranking" or "market rate for human energy" ranking.

Anyway, I'm sure you get the idea by now. Categories all have rankings and there are way too many categories to go into all the details. In case you're interested, People Magazine ranks the "most beautiful people" each year. The point is that you get the idea of the "multi-categorical" score sheet of energy inflows.

Doorway Twenty-Five of reality

Teaching: Stress from the Energy Loss/Gain Perspective

Now that I've trained you in how to look at human energy exchanges and to watch the flow of human energy in every exchange, I will now present the list of things that cause stress in human life. Don't you now see the human energy imbalance that these external events cause? It's all about the transfer of energy. Inflow or Outflow—equilibrium is what we seek and need. The **Root Cause** of All Stress, Guilt, Anxiety, Depression and Conflict in Mankind is the perceived unfair or unequal exchange of human energy.

"Stress" List

1. death of spouse
2. divorce
3. marital separation
4. jail term
5. death of close family member or friend
6. personal injury or illness
7. marriage
8. fired from job
9. marital reconciliation

10. retirement
11. change in health of close family member or friend
12. pregnancy
13. sex difficulties
14. gain of new family member
15. business readjustment
16. change in financial state
17. change of residence, moving
18. change to different line of work
19. change in number of arguments with spouse
20. purchase new residence, mortgage/loan for major purchase
21. foreclosure of mortgage or loan
22. change in responsibilities at work
23. son or daughter leaving home
24. trouble with in-laws
25. outstanding personal achievement
26. spouse begins or stops work
27. begin or end school
28. change in living conditions
29. revision of personal habits
30. trouble with boss
31. change in work hours or conditions
32. death of a pet
33. change in schools
34. change in recreation
35. change in church activities
36. change in social activites
37. mortgage/loan for lesser purchase such as car
38. change in sleeping habits
39. change in number of family get-togethers
40. change in eating habits
41. vacation
42. holidays
43. minor violations of the law

The High Cost of Stress

Everyone knows what stress can do to a person. Relaxation therapies are not the answer. Energy equilibrium is and getting in life what one feels **entitled** to is the whole secret. The exchange need not be completely exact and there is no exact science to figure out an even exchange or not. The measuring stick is how one feels in his or her body. The body is always taking a crude measurement every second of every day. In other words, you can relax all you want, but when the person comes back and faces reality, there must be not only "something" in it for him or her, but "enough" in it for him or her. Each person must listen to their bodies (which have been conditioned by energy) to get an energy in = energy out exchange with life. This is where the answer lies ultimately; not in the non-sensible tranquilizer or anti-depressant business of pill popping. Of course relaxing will help, but entitlement for a certain amount of human energy is the real enemy that is now coming to light.

Doorway Twenty-Six of reality

Teaching: Teaching: All Is Not One

Question: Are All Men Created Equal?
Answer: Many religions talk about how "all is one." We are all the same spirit, etc. There may or may not be spirits (and this will remain forever improvable), but never until now has a theory come out which claims that there is *an order* to all people based on "condensed and released energy" of all the human energy systems. A grand pecking order of energy does in reality exist (the mix of quality and/or quantity). This book is basically the collective subconscious of mankind now becoming conscious. The funny thing about this hierarchy of energy is that people don't know they have more energy than another until they lose it. In other words you truly don't know what you've got until its gone. This is because until you experience the loss or the leakage you feel fine. You don't appreciate the energy you have until you feel the pain of losing it. Then you want it back because the energy was yours to begin with (you were raised with it) and this is when and where your entitlement for it begins. Here we talk openly about this issue, but the view from here is about a hierarchical ranking of "energy" which is initially inflowed from society (how it receives your being) and then manifested by our internal

perceptions in our rankings in the multi-categorical energy inflow score sheet of where we fit in on the hierarchy of life. Other spiritual teachers once again completely miss the boat with regards to this issue, as we have become a society conditioned to believe with nonsensical teachings on how we are all the same spirit etc. While the American political system is founded on this notion, by counting each vote equally in an election, there is some attempt at least to "weight" the states in the Electoral College. Some states are simply worth more and this is kind of what I am talking about. Some people are worth more not because they are "better" human beings it is just that they are holding more condensed and/or released energy in their being. They are simply dealing with life on a higher vibration or frequency than other people are. The whole trick as stated many times now is to play life in equilibrium, in balance of the vibration you are currently on. One must remember that the hierarchy is always changing for most of us, but if you are from a many generation deep "powerful" family then this category will carry your vibration for a good long while. In other words, the more generations deep your "good" family is, the less important all the other categories become. On that same note, the more generations your family has been "low" or not powerful, the harder it becomes to make the other categories more important. In general, it takes many generations to either slowly rise or to slowly slip slide away into the lower ranks of energy class. While it is true that before we are born and after we die we all are made up of the same cosmic stuff, while we are here living, it is apparent that some people perceive themselves as superior (and therefore are) and therefore feel entitled to more than others. Other spiritual teachers completely miss the dynamic of time.

They seem to want us to live as if we are all living one second before we were born and are stuck in that time warp or we are all living one second after we have died. As stated, just before we are born and just after we die, then yes "all is one." However, while we live our lives and actually have to live here on planet earth "all is one" is completely inaccurate with regards to reality. The truth of the matter is, we live in a world that is just the exact opposite of the "all is one" ideal. Instead we live in a world which is "all has an order," or "all has a ranking.'

Evidence

We can clearly see that there is logic and reason in our favor as to why there is a pecking order of energy fields that human beings hold. The reasoning is as follows: Any time a human being pays attention to a who or what, he/she subconsciously or now with reading of this book, feels they deserve a perceived fair exchange of their scarce, finite, ultimately impersonal, ultimately impartial, and ultimately neutral human energy. Example: A therapist listens to you and you owe them money (energy). What determines how much a therapist thinks they "ought" to be or "should be" paid is this: The market *plus their level of entitlement* (credentials etc). This is why they all charge different rates. A therapist who feels entitled to say $200/hr will in fact drop their rates if market conditions demand it (supply and demand). Therefore I do agree, the *main factor* in pricing is "the market," but it is *not the only factor,* as economist will have you falsely believe. Supply and demand *is not* the only dynamic at work. The other factor is pride and entitlement to how one view what is "beneath" them and what is not. Investigating the word entitlement is where all our answers are hiding. This book is in fact about the dirty little word entitlement, and we will now come clean on where this word is hiding with regards to therapists. They are a good example because attention is their business. In a theoretical therapy vacuum, each client should in fact be charged different rates so that the therapist can be in equilibrium based on how bored or interested they are in your particular story. The more boring (the less energy you have for them), the more they should charge you or the more likely they are to fall asleep on you while you are talking. This is because their attention is more work for them (in theory) and is their energy exchange with you. So the more boring you are to them, the more their entitlement for equilibrium will become evident and the more likely they will pretend to actually be paying attention to you. It should be obvious to you that the world works this way in reality, and the only mystery is why nobody else seems willing to write about the truth of reality. It's kind of funny actually because everybody knows what's going on, but nobody wants to publicly admit it. It is as if this book is everyone's collective subconscious now becoming conscious.

This book is theoretical much like Einstein's theories about traveling at the speed of light (which of course nobody could realistically even come close to doing). He stated that time would slow down for the individual as he traveled closer and closer to the speed of light. So my theory is similar. As the individual becomes more and more boring to the therapist, the closer they are to falling asleep on you. If reality really worked properly, we would in theory all be carrying around little energy machine monitors calculating who owes whom what at the end of each exchange. In other words, if you are boring to a therapist and they pay the same amount attention to you as their next client who is extremely engaging—they would have a monitor that that says you owe them more money than the next client. In other words, therapists would all charge a sliding scale based on the inverse proportion to how interesting you actually are to them. The more boring you are, the more expensive the session (holding the attention variable constant).

The point is this as we beat a dead horse here:

All motion has an equal and opposite reaction. Energy is never lost; just transferred around. Remember the Physics chapter—this is an indisputable law of motion (Newton's 3rd law, Einstein, laws of thermodynamics). Therefore each therapist feels their entitlement in their bodies after each session of whether or not it was "worth it" or not. Subconsciously or consciously they will compensate with their attention to you if you're simply not being charged enough. So watch out for sleepy therapists!

SECTION FIVE

A Matter Of Neutrality

Doorway Twenty-Seven of reality

Teaching: Love, Law, "Free" Will, and "Neutral" Energy

In reality where I live, love is a relationship that involves two parties who are in equilibrium with each other as far as human energy exchanges are concerned and all human system conditioning. This is why timing is so important with regards to intimate relationships. Both parties have to be "ready," and timing is a form of energy (see energy forms). Love creates a good feeling inside us because this is the natural selection process telling us that in order for us to increase our chances of survival it is more advantageous for us to be in a partnership with this particular human being. If one perceives that he or she has a greater chance of survival by being alone then this person will have no need for love. Once again, everything we do is defensive, protective, and selfish so that we will not suffer.

Lawsuits

A word about law; Lawsuits are attempts to make a perceived fair exchange of human energy. They happen because something has happened which left someone's perceived human energy in a deficit, loss, or leakage and since life is a competition for this scarce and finite precious resource (energy), the battle in the legal system will begin for equilibrium once again.

Law = Honorable Profession?

I'm sure you know by now that judges raise their hand to God and swear that they will do justice without "respect to persons." Now welcome to the real world. Lawyers know for a fact that corruption is all around them and those who don't admit it have deliberately made themselves blind to it. You see, it's once again all about energy. There are partners who overcharge their clients, partners who have drinks or play golf with the judges so that they can tell their clients that they have the judge "in their pocket." **None of this should really come as a surprise to you.**

I do not consider this theory to be a faith or belief system that people should follow blindly. I believe a full understanding of this book to be practically useful to people so that they can better understand the root cause of stress, anxiety, conflict, and tension in human society. I do not believe this book is "good" or "bad" for human civilization since I do not believe in "good" or "bad" remember. All there is in reality is evolution of consciousness. This is the goal of humanity—evolution into higher states of awareness and consciousness. We must begin to talk about our human experience accurately that's all and to understand that all human life is one energy ball (person) exchanging with another energy ball (another person) or one energy ball (person) exchanging with another energy ball (object, not a person). Most of our energy exchanging comes from other people though we exchange with whatever we pay attention to (movies, books, food etc.) Our energy is hidden behind our earth suits that just so happen to be made out of skin. I encourage people to question every concept written here, and decide for themselves by using the real world as a laboratory. This is what I have done. I ask you to use your power of logic and reason to make your own conclusions about the true nature of reality and the laws of human energy dynamics

Review Time!

The body is inhabited by an energy field (vibe, aura, whatever you want to call it is fine), which is self-created by our internal perceptions of ourselves which is directly connected through our brain (perceptions) to our nervous and all other conditioned human systems. We walk around and interact with this energy field and transfer energy in and out all around us every second of our lives. We must always remember a few laws about energy. Number 1, Energy tends to condense before it releases (think of an avalanche); for every action, there is an equal and opposite reaction, and energy is never lost—just transferred around. We must also be aware that because of the multi-categorical score sheet of self-perception we are all part of one "energy class" or another. The "energy class" that we are in determines our level of entitlement in every single situation. Energy classes are like different ballparks. Different ballparks cannot exchange equally in a social vacuum because the vibration is too different. You must find the people who belong on your wavelength and can sit with you in your ballpark. This is because every second of life is in fact business, the business of human energy competition.

Question: Why is everything *ultimately neutral*? Doesn't your belief in God imply "good" and "evil?"

Answer: Well, since I believe "free" will is an illusion and we are all just fighting over ultimately impersonal, ultimately impartial, and *ultimately neutral* energy, I also therefore believe no human being is ultimately responsible for his or her actions. In other words your path is your path and that is that as you fight for energy and relieve, avoid, eliminate your personal suffering (feels personal, but its just your assignment). Since nobody can prove God has a personality and cares one way or the other about anything, I remain neutral on the matter. In other words—God is just neutral energy that is finite here on earth. The "Big Bang" released by God was just *ultimately neutral* energy and it seeped into mankind. There isn't enough to go around to satisfy each living creature's entitlement issues for equilibrium (safety from suffering).

Question: So you do believe in God?

Answer: Yes. God/Creator/Whatever started everything *is ultimately impersonal, impartial, neutral,* **energy.** This is a spiritual book with spiritual theories and that is why the word *"enlightenment"* is the first word in the title. The word *"enlightenment"* to me just means awareness. The energy released in the "Big Bang" *was and will forever be impersonal*, and seeped into mankind to make us "go." This is what powers us to move around and do things—energy. We are not plugged into a wall outlet for energy or power; we just have it because we were born into this world. "God," if you want to call it that, set in motion physical laws (which we already know about) that control energy systems (Physics) and also hidden laws of energy that control human energy dynamics and systems. They're just hidden, that's all. "God" does not play dice or favorites.

Question: But what if I still believe in "free" will?

Answer: That's great for you. You have these thoughts to create the energy you need to feel best about yourself. Keep in mind, though, the energy is still *ultimately impersonal, impartial, and neutral*. This is why people all have different "energy assignments," and why some people end up in jail or in wars. There is no good and evil, just different "energy assignments," as we compete for this very precious, scarce finite resource. We need energy to survive. There is "will," the will to survive. That's our survival instinct. It just isn't "free" because there are hidden laws at work in all human interactions and behavior. Just as there are physical laws in the physical Universe, there are also human energy laws in the invisible Universe (human behavior). I admit to Law #1 and so should you if you want to awake. In other words, you can believe in whatever you want as long as you agree to law #1. After you admit to law #1 as being truth, then anything goes as far your assignment and belief system go. We will compete for energy that's all with different views on "free" will. Once again, here it is:

Law #1—All human thought and action (including this book) has evolved to be one hundred percent defensive, protective, selfish, and self-serving so that one can avoid, relieve, reduce, or completely eliminate all forms of suffering via a perceived equal and fair exchange of energy. Overall human energy balance (equilibrium) is what we seek and deserve. Human energy imbalance is the *root cause* of all conceivable forms of human suffering and *all mental illnesses*.

Question: What do you mean by "ultimately?"
Answer: The word *ultimately* is up to each of us to define, but I will help you out in this struggle. Think of a sporting event such a boxing or ice hockey. *During the game*, there is extreme violence, fierce competition, and everything feels personal. *After the game*, the players congratulate each other on a hard fought battle and shake hands etc. They kiss and make up basically. So herein lies the secret of life—the dynamic of time with regards to the impersonal. *Ultimately* is defined by you, but the Universe will define it for you if you can't. This is death.
Question: What is my suggestion on the matter?
Answer: Each day is a lifetime. Each morning to around bedtime is the "game." *As we prepare to die (meaning sleep)— the game is over*. Each night when we think about our

day—we must see it as ultimately impersonal, impartial, and neutral. *I have defined ultimately as each day.* You should do whatever works best for you. You can define it by each second, each minute, each hour, daily, weekly, monthly, yearly or whatever works. Keep in mind though; the Universe will *ultimately* define it for you—death.

While not judging people and things sounds great in theory (as other spiritual teachers recommend nonsensically), *in reality* where I live it is not possible. For one thing, in order to be judgeless, one needs to take a stance of an impartial witness where one simply "witnesses" his or her own experience as a neutral observer. In order to actually accomplish this, one must become aware of the constant stream of judging and our normal reactions of our inner and outer experiences that we are caught up in and simply take a step back and simply "observe" them.

This person would then never actually do anything because he or she would be too busy just observing. Our minds as human beings have evolved to order, rank, and make sense out of things . . . *and people.* We can leave our judgments behind when we meditate, but once we are in the "real" world, we cannot help but judge people since our survival instinct is at play. *The real mystery is why other spiritual teachers do not acknowledge ranking and therefore judging people as a reality of normal human existence. The life we live is ultimately impersonal, impartial, and neutral, but we still need to live our lives in the meantime. Other teachers have simply missed the boat with regards to the dynamic of time!*

Doorway Twenty-Eight of reality

Teaching: No such things as Coincidences & Accidents

Coincidences and accidents require a separate discussion all its own because of all the confusion that surrounds these two words. So let's cut to the chase and get right to the teaching on this matter.

Question: Are there such things as coincidences and accidents?
Answer: No. There are no such things in reality. Everything has a cause and an effect. You just don't know all the causes and only see the visible, tangible effects. You only see the vortexes.

Coincidence(s) & Accidents

A coincidence or accident is not God "winking at you" or other nonsensical explanations by other silly spiritual teachers of a "master plan" for you, your life or the Universe. The Celestine Prophecy (the book) simply had it all wrong along with ever other author about reality. God does not care one way or another about what happens on earth because He does not take sides nor play dice. As stated, all He/She/It did was set in motion invisible laws that we must all adhere to. A coincidence is the intersection of many causes and effects and that is all. A coincidence is simply a mathematical improbability. You only see the intersection, but not all the causes and effects that lead up to it. Your SELFISH conditioned nervous system (human system) feels something when a coincidence happens because it is selfishly looking for energy and perceives a big coincidence as "luck" or something divine. However many coincidences happen that you do not feel that "tingling feeling" because it is a coincidence that in your perception will not aid your survival. A human's selfishness is most apparent actually with regards to coincidences. We only claim "it's meant for us," "it's a sign," "it's fate" because we are so damn selfish to feel good. We only see what we want to see as a "divine plan" when it aids us in someway. Some coincidences we ignore, and others we inference some grand cosmic meaning. In reality—a coincidence is a mathematical probability manifesting itself that's all. God does not take sides, play favorites, or care one way or another what happens here on earth because he is a neutral power who set in motion invisible and visible laws and that's that. Your body gravitates towards pleasure and away from pain so the coincidence(s) that one perceives will avoid and/or relieve psychological and/or emotional suffering seem to be the coincidences that we remember and thank God for. On the other hand, just as many coincidences happen that we do not accept because there is no perceived gain "in it" for us. Everybody (except me) is taking life both ways. In other words, people seemingly arbitrarily sometimes call a coincidence "meant for them and that the event was meant to be. But then other times, when the coincidence doesn't serve them in a "good feeling" way, the coincidence means nothing and it does not mean anything in particular is "meant for them" by virtue of the coincidence. So which is it? In a way this is psychological masturbation. "Everything happens for a reason" some of the time at my choosing is what people tell themselves nonsensically and inconsistently. Once again, the selfish conditioned human system only recognizes what it perceives is best for it to do and say and using coincidences as a way for us to feel good about ourselves makes perfect sense. We selfishly tell ourselves that

God is finally providing for us, answering our prayers and showing us "the way." It does make sense to utilize coincidences as energy gains but it has nothing to do with "God's will" for us or that we are being singled out by God to do something over another thing. Our condition nervous system (human system) simply does what it does to feel best about itself which may or may not include recognizing certain coincidences as divine energy or not. Society for some reason loves to believe that God chooses sides and it is subtly played out in daily life. For example, in the movie "Bruce Almighty," God was played by Morgan Freeman and at the end of the movie came out wearing a Yankee hat. There are no words to describe the stupidity of this insinuation on a defenseless public. It was slipped into the movie incognito. It was a subtle display of blasphemy and in terrible taste. I hope the creative team of this movie (Mr. Oedekerk, Mr. Shadyac, Mr. Carrey, and Mr. Freeman) one day read this teaching and understand the enormity of their subtle stupidity. I have a feeling they felt it was cute etc. and would somehow sell more movie tickets since there are so many Yankee fans and/or so many people who want a divine explanation to why the Yankees have won so many times over the last one hundred years. *You simply cannot put a baseball hat on God and imply that he prefers one thing (team) to another.* This crosses a huge line. At the very least why not put an Angels hat on God? Even that would've been too stupid for words but at least the idea of Angels would have been construed. The constant barrage of media implications that God takes sides in life is utterly ridiculous and offensive to people who are sensitive to truth. Let's get this straight once and for all. God is neutral and created neutral energy on earth. "Positive" and "negative" experiences are in the eyes of the beholder and no one has the final say on what is "good" or "bad" for another human being or society at large. All we have is evolution of consciousness. Period.

Question: But wasn't JFK jr.'s death an airplane accident?
Answer: No. Many contributing factors caught up to him. Your subconscious will always catch up to you. Every slip

of the tongue (Freud got something correct) means something that is in your subconscious. JFK Jr. flew at night and was not night rated. Obviously some sort of death wish was in him and he was a ticking time bomb. Subconsciously, his life was over and had no meaning. Perhaps he secretly felt—he has lost the love he once felt for his wife and/or his magazine wouldn't make it and therefore he had nothing in life left "to do." Since he couldn't check into a psych ward due to his fame or commit suicide due to his fame, he led a dangerous lifestyle that was buried in his subconscious of an energy form that has nothing left.

Question: So what happened to him once he died?

Answer: The energy he held in his body—his condensed energy otherwise known as internal perceptions was released back into the Universe where it started. The released energy in his life (and there was a lot of it) had already been released so that energy was being transferred around. His internal perceptions of himself were condensed at the time of his death and since all perceiving ends when you die; it gets released back into the Universe. The more energy you released and/or condensed in your lifetime will force attention onto you by your death. In other words—the more powerful you are (good or evil doesn't matter) is the amount of attention you get by the alive *energy standard people* when you die (quality and quantity of attention remember).

Doorway Twenty-Nine of reality

Teaching: The Country Club

As I sit at a very exclusive Manhattan area private beach club, my mind once again ponders the true nature of reality. I'm quite sure of my theories now so I think I'll write a book explaining them all. Once people fully understand them, I hope people (other than me) will see the world as I do and understand where entitlement feelings come from.

As I sit here at the "beach club" and ponder its "energy field," I give thanks to the universe for granting me the opportunity to reveal the true nature of reality (laws of human energy dynamics) through this book. The universe is using my nervous system to write this book for the world and therefore it is my assignment to do so. We are doing this together. This is why it's ultimately impersonal energy that's writing it. Anyway, I sit here with all this physical beauty around me, surrounded by high-energy class people, and feel it is my duty, my obligation to this world to finally come clean as to how the world really works. I'm quite sure I have or "we" have uncovered hidden universal truths about mankind and how he functions while we are here on earth.

I look up and see the expensive boats on Long Island Sound. I see the sailboats. I see the Manhattan and Connecticut elite here and wonder can anybody see what I see? Am I the only one on this planet uniquely gifted to understand what really causes tension in the nervous system? Is every spiritualist and religion wrong? Is every philosophy off the mark? Is every psychoanalyst, psychiatrist, and every other mental health professional missing the boat? I say yes.

As I sit here, it becomes harder and harder for me to figure out why I'm the only person to my knowledge that sees things as they truly are. My only explanation is actually threefold: (1) that based on my karmic path this is how my nervous system will unleash the energy it holds to achieve the relaxation/peace of mind it is entitled to; (2) my nervous system needs to receive back the energy needed to relax the nervous system via a perceived fair exchange of energy; (3) my theories are very "unpolitically correct" and the few people who could've written about this same topic don't want to admit to themselves that it's okay for people to feel "better" or "superior" than other people, and therefore feel entitled to more energy in return.

According to me (we)—the earth has finite human energy (seeped into mankind from Big Bang). This energy is all around us, but humans only have a *finite* amount. All living and non-living things compete for this energy. For the purposes of this book, we will stick with humans and human energy. This *ultimately impersonal* human experience we are having is clearly a competition for energy. Our lives unfold in a one-thing-leads-to-another karmic stream as we use our supercomputer brains/intellect/intuition to make decisions that we perceive will give us the fairest exchange of our energy. It's so clear to me it's scary. If you don't have the energy you need or perceive you need, you will be tense and nervous. Relaxation is the goal and can only be achieved in emotional states of perceived fair energy exchanges. I hope you are no longer confused about this difficult subject matter, but are you nervous or relaxed as you read this? If you're nervous, then you are in energy deficit right now in your life and/or are not exchanging fairly with this text.

I will close with this chapter with imagery. I sit here on a beautiful beach facing many sailboats on the Long Island Sound on a beautiful, hot, clear, sunny day in June with a warm breeze. The beach club is a big beautiful salt water pool behind me with a snack bar, ice cream stand, a full bar with televisions and locker rooms. The people I see are from the rarefied environment, the "elite" of New York and Connecticut. I see families and hear the sound of the waves. I feel the hot sun warming my body all over. It is clear to me sitting here that we, humans, are in a fierce competition and getting fiercer and fiercer as populations increase. This is why I say the energy we compete for is "scarce." It simply feels scarce and when you stop and think what some people are willing to do for love or money, I'm sure you'll agree.

We will compete for love, compassion, understanding, hope, attention, money, food, etc., as the survival instinct takes over. This is because as humans we need human energy to survive. This is because we take up space in the Universe and by doing so need energy to eat and shelter ourselves. We are balls of energy concealed by a mask (our skin). Saying energy is infinite is like saying and denying we live in a capitalistic society and that society will not take advantage of us if you feel entitled to nothing and simply get your energy and good feelings from nature and God only. God may be infinite, but our *attention to Him is finite.* In other words, God must compete with us for our attention just like movies, books, TV, and radio, etc. Eventually when it's your turn to pay the bill, and you perceive it is unfair for you to do so, will your survival instinct (nervous system) react painfully. Only when you perceive it (energy) comes out of your pocket (tank) unfairly, will you feel the energy loss. This is when one bleeds invisible energy.

Doorway Thirty of reality

Teaching: Needs Versus Wants Explained

What one needs in life with regards to energy is subjective and different for each individual. No one can say what another person needs when it comes to this invisible force secretly controlling everything. Only the body knows because the nervous system is where the truth is stored via **a conditioned nervous system. Buddha, like all teachers before me had it wrong:** The so called "middle path" is the one Buddha said to take. The "middle path" relative to who or what? One man's "middle path" (to have servants, etc.) may be another man's "high path." Buddha also said that perception isn't reality. He couldn't have been farther from the truth. Perception *is* reality. This is because our brain controls our nervous system and our perceptions control our brain.

The fine line between wants and "needs" is easily explainable now. The nervous system will react painfully when energy "needs" are not met. Nobody really knows what they "need" in advance. However, once one feels the painful feelings associated with human energy imbalance disorder will he or she realize that his or her unique individual needs are not being met. If "needs" are not being met and it is not possible to acquire what one needs, a nervous breakdown, crime, or some sort of "lashing out" will result which will in turn force the issue as the body will force attention to it (energy) to make the exchange a perceived fair one again. It is very dangerous to condition the nervous system "expensively," or with a lot of energy inflows because there is a much greater chance to not get what one "needs" when the energy source is depleted (there is much more room on the downside).

Doorway Thirty-One of reality

Teaching: Other Spiritual Teachers

It is as if other spiritualists want us to pretend that we do not live here on planet earth for zero—one hundred twenty years. They want us to live in the "all is one" model of the Universe, which is a silly, unattainable, and grossly unrealistic ideal at best. All evidence clearly states that there is a hierarchical order to all of mankind based on his internal perceptions of himself or herself and others. We know for a fact that there a princes and peasants and everything in between. We know that there are co-op boards, country club admission committees, and universities that are nearly impossible to get into. We know certain nightclubs only allow certain people in based on physical appearances, etc. We know colleges have fraternities and sororities that only allow certain types of people in. We know escorts exist and charge different prices for sexual contact. We sense a great pecking order out there, but are afraid to acknowledge it. We are afraid to admit that all is not one. We know it's "all has an order."

People don't like to admit openly that they feel "superior" or "better" than another person. It's life's dirty little secret. The truth of the matter is that people are not "better" or "superior" to others, but people do perceive themselves as such. Perception is reality. As stated earlier, what you perceive is directly tied into your nervous system, which directly affects your exchanges as you compete for scarce, finite, ultimately impersonal, impartial, neutral human energy.

When one is constantly leading himself or herself to relieve and/or avoid psychological and/or all conceivable human suffering, the whole notions of altruism and/or "selflessness" go straight out the window. Hello, Darwin! Darwinism is simply survival of the fittest, but he never spoke about it in human energy terms. The tricky part about energy survival and natural selection this way is that we must understand that each human being needs a different amount of energy to survive (based on entitlement issues) because if not, he or she will get extremely depressed, agitated, anxious and may end up committing suicide.

Nervous system pain is real (anxiety). Nervous system pleasure is real (relaxation). These are truths. Our bodies can sense a loss of energy and this is painful because our survival instinct takes over. Our bodies recognize energy and want and demand for us to get our fair exchanges. The body feels entitled to a perceived fair exchange of energy. The nervous system is the keeper of the truth because it has been conditioned and bred with energy inflows.

Question: What's the goal of thinking?
Answer: The goal of all thought is risk assessment. We think so much so we can decide what is overall best for us to do so that we can feel the best about ourselves, psychologically and/or emotionally. The mind is constantly assessing risk of psychological and/or emotional injury. Every decision, every thought, is a constant "sizing up" of possibilities of how one can avoid psychological injury. Risk assessment is the answer to why everyone thinks so much. Should I do this or should I do that? Over and over again. The reasons why are the reasons of how we can survive that moment, that situation, with the least amount of psychological/emotional suffering or with the most amount of psychological/emotional "good feeling." So we are either trying to make ourselves feel "less bad" or make ourselves feel "most good" at every moment of existence.

Doorway Thirty-Two of reality

Teaching: Some More Questions Answered

Question: "What is narcissism?
Answer: Narcissism is a feature of our survival instinct. We need narcissism to survive. You see it in infants who not only are demanding that their needs be met but also are fascinated by their own bodies. It is how we discover who we are and what we need. Therapists tell us extreme narcissism is a bad thing and even call it a personality disorder. They say it exists when our own needs exclude the desire and/or capacity to care for others. But what if the narcissist is simply adhering to esoteric universal truth? What if the narcissist is superior because he perceives this to be so and can prove more condensed energy in fact conditioned his nervous system. Why should the narcissist experience energy leakage/loss disorder and bleed the most precious prized resource on earth? Therefore, the narcissist would in fact feel more *entitled* to energy than the next guy. If my theory is in fact truth, then people need to understand that all the so-called "narcissist" is trying to do in life is avoid/relieve psychological and/or emotional suffering just like everybody else is doing. The only difference is that he or she is operating in life at a higher level and this is why he or she feels entitled to more. When people

around the narcissist sense his or her entitlement for energy, they tend to fight back the only way they can—calling him or her insulting names. Bleeding invisible energy is extremely painful and happens at every level of society. This is where entitlement comes from. Entitlement is born out of the desire to not bleed energy and can you blame someone for not wanting to suffer? The problem in life always arises when two or more people feel entitled to the same thing—energy. This is where the battlefield of life is. The fierce and brutal competition for energy is the true nature of reality. *There isn't enough to go around and many people feel entitled to it (energy of course) by virtue of their births.*

Question: What was before the Big Bang? Before the Origination Point?

Answer: I'm neither God, nor the Son of God (neither was Jesus), and I have no idea nor is it relevant to our discussions. Before the Big Bang, nobody will ever know what went on. The instant *after* the Big Bang is what I claim to understand better than any human being as the ultimately impersonal, impartial, neutral energy was released into the Universe. Energy was released that's all and I'm just the messenger who is reporting that not enough seeped into mankind to please everyone. Energy in the universe is a scientific provable fact. In fact all living and non-living things compete for this scarce and finite precious resource.

Question: Why is everything perceived? Why not just say there is a *truth* to every category?

Answer: There is probably, but as far as feelings of entitlement go, if you perceive yourself a certain way, you create energy for yourself. If for some odd reason you have beliefs about yourself that are totally off the mark, you'll still believe you have a right to more human energy. Perceptions are part of reality, and *the truth* is about how feelings of entitlement and superiority exist and must be understood in society (because perception is part of being a normal human being). Perceptions of how you rank in the categories of life give you your energy. If you are considered by society to be extremely ugly, but you think you're beautiful, you still have your human energy for this category to work with. Having a gross misperception is extremely rare due to the fact that if your perceptions are way off the mark (and society is the judge), it will be nearly impossible to maintain as you interact with the world. The reason for this is the simple fact that the nervous system will validate or invalidate your perception as you meet other people in life. This point is now clear.

Question: Don't people already know that superiority complexes exist?

Answer: Yes, they do, but it almost always is one or two-dimensional. In other words one race or religion looks down on another race or religion etc. What I'm bringing to light here is that real entitlement comes from energy inflows into possibly hundreds of categories. The real order in the energy hierarchy comes from many categories and race/religion are just two of them and in my view have no inherent ranking (like all categories it's all up to your perception). My perception is that a person's skin/race or religion can affect his or her perceptions a certain way though and make them feel more or less entitled to energy. It depends on how they view their personal experiences throughout life as their nervous system gets conditioned (all human systems but its easier to just say nervous system) based on their race or religion etc. I believe that many people feel entitled to the same thing (need I tell you at this stage it is human energy we are fighting for), and this is why conflict is inevitable. As stated previously, I believe there simply isn't enough to go around and this is the inherent competitive nature of reality. For someone to be truly "superior," they need to be like "the perfect storm." So this means on average, you score highly in like hundreds of categories. To feel "better" than someone based on race or religion alone is one-dimensional and is the viewpoint of a very unaware or unenlightened person. The point of this book/philosophy/theory is to enlightened people after all of what *the root cause* of stress and conflict is. Now people tend to date people of their same race and religion because there is simply more energy there. Remember—understanding is energy.

Question: Is the energy still releasing/expanding? Is it finite or infinite?

Answer: Listen up and listen good. It's not relevant. We humans have energy and *we humans are finite* (we know we will die and have timelines to our lives). Even when we die, and our energy goes back to the universe, this particular incarnation will be over. Since we are finite, our energy currency as human beings is also finite (our attention). The money supply can be increased and this just makes a new finite level. Populations are also increasing, making it even more competitive and fierce.

Question: Why was the energy released by God (insert whatever you call this power here if you like)?

Answer: I don't know why or how, nor do I care. Energy was released into the Universe and that is a provable scientific fact. The energy was impersonal, impartial and neutral to begin with and will be to end with. "Positive" and "negative" experiences that people have with life are all a matter of individual perspectives relative to the "neutral source" of energy inherent in the Universe. People filter it based on their feelings towards the external events that happen to them. If it feels "bad" then it's "negative" and if it feels "good" then it's a "positive" experience. This is a more reasonable theory than believing God cares about what happens here on earth because nobody can prove God has a personality, and cares either way what you do with your life. It is not "good" or "evil" energy— it's just energy. It makes more sense to believe that we need energy to live and we are all fighting over this scarce invisible resource. If feels "good" to attain energy and "bad" to leak or lose it because our survival instinct knows what is needs to survive.

Question: What do I believe in regard to Jesus, the Bible, and other religious scriptures?

Answer: Jesus most likely existed but was not the "son of God"—he was just a powerful person with energy that needed to be released. The same goes for any other famous person in history. As far as all the stories in the Old and New Testament and other religious scriptures, they all remain as of these writings scientifically improvable. I understand my theories are also improvable, but I believe *less improvable* than a God that takes sides, plays dice and has favorites. There is no absolute authority on anything since God *is* impersonal, impartial and neutral energy that we fight for.

Question: What is social anxiety disorder and anxiety in general?

Answer: Anxiety is simply the feeling of bleeding invisible energy (being in energy leakage/loss). It is the body's way of telling us that what we are paying attention to is not giving us a perceived fair exchange of energy in return. It's actually a simple concept after all. This is our nervous system telling us not to get into certain situations again because we need to hold onto our scarce finite energy. This is why we are on a blind, trial and error, positive and negative, nervous system assignment or energy assignment. One must remember that all human conflict *(internal or external conflict)* comes from a perceived unfair exchange of energy.

Question: What are depression and bipolar depression?

Answer: Depression is simply energy leakage/loss disorder. Bipolar is simply the patient going *in and out of* energy leakage/loss disorder or gaining or surging too much energy that he or she doesn't know what to do with it all (can't process it fast enough). One needs to feel there is enough "in it" for him or her. Not just something "in it" for him/her, *but enough*. The word enough is also where entitlement is hiding since we all have different views of what *enough* means. When one has their perceived fair exchange of energy, they feel better (bipolar and depression explained). This is why depressed people move slower—they are trying to match and come into equilibrium with the amount of energy they have. Humans can leak/lose/bleed energy one second and gain it the next. It's a moment-to-moment thing.

Question: Does therapy work with regards to the true nature of reality and laws of human energy dynamics?

Answer: No, not yet anyway. The reason why psychiatrists, psychologists and social workers do not see the true nature of reality is this: Doctors in the mental health field in general wear compensating blinders and have tunnel vision only in what they have studied and know about. This is human nature and makes perfect sense. You cannot diagnose someone with something that has not been invented yet. This is the first book in history describing life this way. So if you are currently in treatment and want the doctor to understand you better, and believe in this book, then make them read it!

Question: What are Energy Vampires?

Answer: Some people, by their very presence, seem to drain the energy of those unprotected people around them.

This simply means they have less energy than you (in your perception) and *you are paying attention to them.* Your nervous system will fire the alarm and alert you to this perceived unfair exchange of energy. The next time you see this person (if you have something else better to do), you will not give them your scarce energy (attention). If you have nothing else better to pay attention to *and still* hang out with this inferior person or thing, you will see that the opportunity cost (what you would be doing if you were not with this person) is lower (boredom etc.). So the superior person may in fact pay attention to an inferior person because he has nothing else better to do. This can then become the fairest exchange available to him or her at that time. On the other hand, if you see a perceived inferior person or thing, just don't pay that much attention to them (it). Let them pay attention to you. As you now know, attention is the currency of energy.

Doorway Thirty-Three of reality

Teaching: Selflessness Does Not Exist

Do not believe in the virtue of selflessness. This is a lie. A dirty lie put forth by society as an ideal without thought to its attainability. No human being will ever be selfless. They will tell you they are being selfless. Church sermons will preach selflessness. Even Buddha talked nonsensically about its virtues. There is a higher truth that must be known and in fact it is Law #1 of this book. Once again here it is:

Law #1—All human thought and action (including this book) has evolved to be one hundred percent defensive, protective, selfish, and self-serving so that one can avoid, relieve, reduce, or completely eliminate all forms of suffering via a perceived equal and fair exchange of energy. Overall human energy balance (equilibrium) is what we seek and deserve. Human energy imbalance is the **root cause** of all conceivable forms of human suffering and **all mental illnesses**.

Law #1 explains "self-destructive" and suicidal behavior.

So I don't care if you do charity work, go to church, are a "good person," etc. I don't care if you are Mother Teresa—you have kids, don't have kids, are an "enlightened" Buddhist Monk, are a famous spiritual teacher, or whatever it is you think you are doing to "help other people. We are all doing the same exact thing—avoid and/or relieve psychological and/or emotional suffering.

The bullshit out there is simply incredible to watch as a brainwashed person thinks they are selfless in the name of being a "good person." Yes, you can be "selfless," then you have no ego and have nothing "in it" for you at all. This is called being a martyr, which is suicide anyway while you are in physical form. The only problem with this is that *nobody is a martyr. This should not come as a surprise to you: Even the martyr isn't a martyr. Psychology is always behind it.*

Doorway Thirty-Four of reality

Teaching: Use Your Intelligence

Intelligence is used when something from the outside world is presented to it for the purpose of determining how much "truth" is in it. Humans most often believe that truth is simply a matter of personal opinion when it comes to the truths discussed here in this book. I want to make clear that this book does in fact claim that what is presented here are in fact esoteric laws that secretly guide all human interactions. This is why the laws of physics as they pertain to energy systems were discussed previously. All one has to do is simply test the laws in a laboratory. This laboratory does in fact exist. This laboratory is called planet earth and all one needs to do is simply sit back and observe human behavior. You will notice that if you use the laws outlined here as a guide, you will quickly see that beneath all known and obvious interactions, that the universal laws of human energy dynamics always hold true. Science and math can prove many truths and theorems on the basis that they have provable quantitative formulas that will hold true or not. When it comes to human behavior, all we can do and hope for is to observe life and make as much sense out of it as humanely possible. This book has the theories to do just that, and does in fact claim to be the closest possible explanation of reality currently in print.

Question: If there is no "right" or "wrong" as you claim, why do you claim this book is "right?"

Answer: "Right and wrong" with regards to what you do with your life ultimately does not exist and I am one hundred percent consistent. With regards to this text, I do believe in "true and false" (and every nuance in between) with regards to reality. True and false have very different meanings than right, wrong, good, or evil. I am simply writing a book that I believe to be true, and I am arguing the points so that you can see it as truth also.

Doorway Thirty-Five of reality

Teaching: Yankee Stadium and Energy

Another example of energy would be for a kid to grow up playing little league baseball on the Yankee Stadium field—this field, this special place, is a type of energy (atmosphere) that is bred into him (his conditioned human systems). In other words, the air he breathes on this field is in effect and with regards to his upbringing "expensive air." There is a lot of energy on that field because so many people pay *attention* to what goes on there. To every other kid this is sacred ground. If other "regular" kids who were not "fortunate" enough to have ever played on this magical field heard their league championship game was to be played on this field they would all be very excited from the time they heard this news to the day of the game. But for the one kid who grew up playing on the field, he won't be so excited. He grew up playing on that field and this attention or energy (space, atmosphere etc.) then became invested in him. It's just like growing up in an expensive neighborhood. An expensive neighborhood also has "expensive air, "expensive atmosphere" and especially "expensive conditioned people all around you the theory states. The energy of that neighborhood gets invested in you as you condense the energy into you conditioned human systems. Anyhow back to the kid; this kid, who grew up playing on the Yankee Stadium field, when it's championship game time, he'll just think to himself "its just the regular field I grew up playing on, what's the big deal about it?" The exchange for him will be that he won't be so excited to play there (he grew up playing on it!). The other kids will feel lucky to play there and will receive a good feeling or a perceived equal exchange of energy (people feel entitled to some luck in their lives). When one gets overly excited (manic), this is just an individual's body trying desperately to find equilibrium energy once again. The body is an energy-balancing machine and if over-flowing with energy, the body needs to either show external signs of this imbalance to make a balance or guilt will settle in (more than one feels entitled to).

Doorway Thirty-Six of reality

Teaching: "Who knows what is good or bad?"

There is an old Chinese story that is paraphrased here: There is a man who loses his horse. His neighbors stop by to say how sorry they are about his loss. But the man says, "Who knows what is good or bad?" Then one day, the horse returns with a pack of wild horses. Again his neighbors stop by to congratulate him on his fortune. The man only says, "who knows what is good or bad?" The man's son decides to break in one of the wild horses, and while doing so, he falls and breaks his leg. The neighbors send their sympathy for the injury, but the man says, "who knows what is good or bad?" When the army comes to recruit soldiers for the war, the man's son is excused from going because of his leg. The neighbors, whose sons have all gone off to war, tell the man how lucky he is, but all the man says is, "who knows what is good or bad?"

Life is a persistent, consistent, positive and negative, trial and error, inevitable changing flow. Unquestionably, the sensitive human brain adds a lot to the richness of life. But this is the price we pay for intelligence! And for this, we pay dearly because, ironically, the increase in overall sensitivity makes us way peculiarly vulnerable.

There can be no doubt that the power to remember things and also the power to predict and make an ordered sequence out of a bunch of helter-skelter chaotic disconnected moments is a wonderful development of human sensitivity. In a way, it is the achievement of the human brain, giving humans the most extraordinary powers of survival and adaptation to life.

The Universe, our genetics, and the society we grew up in condition our human energy systems to eventually create a world in which the fair an equal exchange of human energy (an exchange in equilibrium according to all involved) is constantly sought. We must always remember that energy is never lost; just transferred around. The cosmos' assignment is for each being to relieve, reduce, avoid, or eliminate all forms of conceivable suffering at all costs (including life itself if necessary). The conditioned human energy systems interconnect us all, and this is what drives us to do what we do. The nervous system etc. gets conditioned as we go through life in a cause and effect logarithm, which creates formulas deep inside us for predictability.

The Universe is an extraordinary large place. When we think about the billions of stars and billions of galaxies and the millions of light years between them, one cannot help but be awed at its awesome vastness. And this is only the observable Universe. We are spiritual. We have the right to believe in whatever we want. I believe this book is the beginning of a mass movement towards reality. This emerging field of human energy dynamics will overhaul the entire mental health profession.

Section Six

A Matter Of Evolution

Doorway Thirty-Seven of reality

Teaching: Honestly speaking, how to get better and evolve

Honesty requires the ability to separate in your own mind what you believe to be true from what you wish to be true. All parts of this philosophy/theory are compatible and consistent, and lock together when you look at it from all its angles. It's like a properly completed crossword puzzle; the answers that go across fit with the answers that go down.

Before now, people were unable to figure our why things happen. Now they see that feelings of entitlement are behind everything. This is why I call this book **Enlightenment through Entitlement.**

Objective Truth versus opinion or beliefs are truths which all different types of people from all different walks of life can see it objectively. In other words—a test can be done that proves it. Yes, this means math and science. Where is the proof, the evidence that mental illness is caused by faulty serotonin and other various chemicals in the brain? We've waited long enough for this scientific proof while in the meantime drug companies are getting richer and richer with this outlandish, improvable theory. Once again, my scientific proof is simple and here it is again in case you have forgotten:

My assumption: Human beings are energy machines. Human energy is used when we pay attention to a who or a what (anything doesn't matter). Human beings are not one hundred percent energy efficient so some work done (energy) is lost. This "lost" work is of course not really "lost" because energy can never in reality be "lost." In Physics this is usually called friction. Anyway in human beings this "lost" work is found in human emotion and moods (feeling just okay, better, or worse). Just as there are simple and complex machines and everything in between, human beings have the same rang from simplicity to complexity. Any imbalance in the machine (human) will cause suffering. The machine only works properly in equilibrium, as the machine (human) only wants the amount of energy he or she feels entitled to. Each machine has a different point of equilibrium based on prior conditioning.

Science

Many different scientists from different times in history have all proven the same thing over and over again mutually exclusively. Whether or not you want to study on your own in more detail Sir Isacc Newton, Albert Einstein, Stephen Hawking, or learn more about the Laws of Thermodynamics on your own is up to you. But the upshot is always the same: energy is never lost, cannot be destroyed, and is simply transferred around. All action has an equal and opposite reaction, and energy tends to condense before it releases (this is the nature of energy)—like an avalanche. But if you cannot handle the truth—then maybe it is now time to honor the other side of this debate. Here is an article I found just so we can hear both sides of the same discoveries

Question: How does one cure "human energy imbalance disorder"?
Answer: Go where you feel you need to go to meet the people you need to meet. Listen to your body very carefully. All the answers are in there. The trajectory of your life is already in place, but you must take a neutral attitude about it. All you are doing is evolving to do what you must do to get energy equilibrium. Nothing

is "better" or "worse" than something else. All lives are fascinating and even if you end up committing suicide at the very least find it fascinating and interesting that this was ultimately your neutral assignment in the eyes of the Universe. All paths end up the same—ultimately neutral. A peasant's suicide is just "right" or "wrong" as me writing this book. The vibration or frequency of the assignment is the only thing that makes us different. Ultimately higher frequency assignments get the reward of power and influence over other human beings and lower assignments do not. However—since peace of mind is the endgame—ultimately we are all after the same exact thing on different energy levels with different needs for equilibrium this point is now clear. You must go about your life aware you are searching for energy so that means everything you do is with non-attachment to the ultimate outcome (not the initial outcome) and without judging what happens to you *ultimately*. Your assignment may be to end up in jail or a psych ward for a while. It really doesn't matter what happens to you because your human energy systems will get conditioned or reconditioned for its energy-seeking path. Wherever you go, you are meant to be there as your nervous system etc. gets conditioned on its path to condense and release its energy. Always remember life is ultimately impersonal, ultimately impartial and ultimately neutral. It's just a very competitive world out there and be aware of what people are competing for—energy; human energy.

Question: What do I think of people like Hitler, Stalin, Saddam Hussein, or Osama Bin Laden?

Answer: It's all a matter of perspective. These are/were people who were simply born into their condition nervous (all human energy) system assignments and fulfilled their trajectories as best as they knew how to via perceived fair and equal exchanges of their condensed energy. *These people were simply trying to avoid, relieve, reduce, or eliminate their own personal suffering selfishly.* Guess what? *We are all doing the same exact thing. We all carry the same exact secret.*

As one thing leads to another you will see that ultimately everything comes down to this:

It's my God versus your God and my higher truth (morality) versus yours. Bush honestly believes that God plays favorites and prefers America for some reason and that we (Americans) are the holders of *absolute* and higher truth. Every ruler feels the same way and this is why conflict (war) is inevitable. To understand the mystery of reality, simply look to law #1 as your main rule of thumb. I know I keep repeating it, but its so vital to understanding reality that's it's worth repeating over and over again.

What I hope for is the evolution of mankind so that we can talk accurately about what we are experiencing here on planet earth. Let future leaders declare war on rival nations by simply stating, "this war is about our selfish desire for scarce, finite human energy that we feel we are entitled to (as a collective nation). We believe we are not getting our perceived fair and equal exchange with this nation (Iraq etc.) and now must do what all selfish human beings do; we must fight for equilibrium energy in our nation's collective perception."

To be clear

Everyone seems to think God is on "his or her side." Isn't it clear now how ridiculous this brainwashing is? Isn't clear God does not take sides? Until it is proven that God has a personality, and actually cares about what happens here on earth, my theories will stand superior to the ridiculous notion of "Good" versus "Evil." **IT'S A MATTER OF PERSPECTIVE.** Once again, what we are competing for is a perceived fair exchange of scarce, finite, ultimately impersonal, ultimately impartial, and ultimately neutral human energy? The perceived fair exchange is different for each individual, each company, and each nation. Ultimately though it's an individual energy system matter. Everyone does what they do because they *perceive it's best for him or her at the time*. Osama, Saddam, Bush, Hitler, Stalin—all did/do the same things as we do. We are all human beings and do the same exact things at different levels of energy needs on the inherent energy hierarchy of life. We are conditioned a certain way, to see things from a certain perspective, and want/demand that our energy assignments get fulfilled—to get a perceived fair exchange *and credit* for who they (we) think we/they are/were. All of mankind is afraid of invisible energy imbalance due to the incredible suffering that goes with it (especially the more common bleeding of energy disorder).

God simply set in motion physical and esoteric hidden laws for human behavior (laws of human energy dynamics) and released the invisible energy that we compete for. Our assignments are energy assignments running through our conditioned nervous (energy) systems. We could not choose our parents or genetics, and this is when the conditioning started. If you argue that we did choose our parents, this was still a one-thing-led-to-another trajectory from our past life. Our energy from our previous life came in conditioned to see things a certain way and still needs to release its energy (get its perceived fair exchange). This is why some children just may love to play the piano or whatever appears to be a "natural gift" or a "calling" out of nowhere. In other words, they came into this life previously conditioned in their human energy systems (DNA/genetics). Either way, we are all one hundred percent selfish to get our perceived fair exchanges as we continue on our trajectories.

Question: What happens when we die?
Answer: The greatest unsolved mystery on earth will now be

solved scientifically. As we already have learned, many scientists have *proved* with many different experiments at different times that *energy can never be destroyed*. It is simply transferred around. Since we human beings are energy machines, all we do is condense and release energy. Think of yourself as a ball of energy concealed in an earth suit that just so happens to be made out of skin. During our lives we release energy and that gets transferred around. When we die, all the perceiving obviously ends because we are no longer alive to perceive anything. The internal perceptions (mass) that we have of ourselves die with us. These internal perceptions have created theoretical mass or condensed energy in our conditioned human systems (and this is where it is stored). When you die, your condensed energies (your internal perceptions of yourself and what you deserve) get released back to where it came from—society and/or the Universe. Upon your death, the energy you are holding will release back to where it came from and then gets transferred all around again.

Doorway Thirty-Eight of reality

Teaching: How to feel better part two

This book most of all is about what causes stress, anxiety, tension, and conflict in people. To simplify things, let's just call all these above conditions "stress." Stress originates from many different sources on a multiplicity of levels. We all have our own version of it. The way each of us reacts to certain external "stressors" or "stimuli" is different, and this is a fact, but nobody seems to know why.

The stress I am talking about is not the extreme stressors, which if not avoided will certainly destroy life regardless of how we perceive them. Among these are exposure to bombs, fires, chemical warfare, radiation, or being hit by a spray of bullets that destroy vital organs. At the other end of the spectrum, there are "stimuli" that impinge on us on a daily basis that nobody will find particularly stressful such as gravity. Since gravity is always affecting us, we tend not to notice it. However, if you work for eight to twelve hours standing in one place you will be aware of gravity as a stressor.

Anyway, this book is about the vast middle range of stressors where exposure is neither immediately lethal like bullets flying towards your head nor basically benign like gravity. The stress this book is about is psychological and emotional stress, which is directly tied to how you perceive other people, other things and yourself. Many silly psychotherapists, doctors and spiritualists will say "you have the power to control the stress you feel by simply handling it better and or willing yourself into saying different things to yourself. You can do such things as breathe deeply, etc." I say this is not true. Energy comes into you and/or out of you, and the imbalance you feel is simply a truth. The energy imbalance must be treated as a truth in the Universe.

Let's take an example.

To make this simple, say, person A is a prince from a royal family and person B is a peasant.

The prince and the peasant both went to a supermarket to buy food and only expected to wait in line for ten minutes. They had been to this supermarket a hundred million times before and the wait was always no more than ten minutes. Their conditioned human energy systems (especially the nervous system in this case) had been conditioned for a ten-minute wait. Now on this particular day, the line was at least three hours long. Now one person (person A) is getting very upset, tense, and anxious while another one (person B) is not. Why?

As stated—silly psychotherapists, doctors and spiritual teachers all say the same incorrect things that completely ignore the inherent hierarchical structure of reality. Why they continue to completely miss the boat with regards to reality is the real mystery here.

Now back to reality:

One of the main points of this book is to understand that the "energy class" (multi-categorical score-sheet overall score for entitlement feelings) of the person getting more upset (person A) is in his perception higher than the person who is not getting upset (person B). In other words, the Universe has created a world in which attention is the currency of energy and person A is simply leaking/losing more energy than person B even though the amount of time on the line is exactly the same. Why?

Prince A's **attention is in reality more valuable** than Peasant B's and that is why Prince A is more upset in this situation. Prince

A IS LEAKING/LOSING/BLEEDING more invisible energy than his fellow man Peasant B. Prince A's nervous system and all conditioned human energy systems have had higher energy inflows into it them (making them a "more expensive," or more valuable overall system). The frequency that Prince A's life is on is higher than that of Peasant B's that's all. Therefore it is easy to conclude that "all is not one" as Prince A has less tolerance for wasting his energy because it is of a higher grade. The gas inside Prince A is grade 93 while Peasant B's gas is grade 87. In other words, in this small example, we see that the laws of human energy dynamics hold because people's attention are not equally valuable. This is real life while we are living.

Ultimately, Prince A and Peasant B are equal because all assignments are ultimately neutral (one second after death). The only difference is how much power and influence one has over others while chasing the endgame of peace of mind. Both humans, Prince A and Peasant B shoot for peace of mind; it's just that Prince A needs more energy to attain it (his fair exchange, his equilibrium is so much higher that's all). While we are living one must accept that there are different energy frequencies of life. People emanate different grades and different amounts of human energy that other humans feed off of. It's all about human energy.

The solutions are first and foremost to become aware of reality and what is actually going on. Abandon all your previous notions about what causes stress. What causes stress is "human energy imbalance disorder" which is different for everyone in every different situation. The human body contains all the truth.

As theorized previously:

Not only do people need something "in it" for them, but they in fact need "enough in it" for them. The "enough" part is where entitlement, energy class, and the laws of human energy are hiding. The less "enough" that is "in it" for them, the more stress they will feel. One can try to "remove or transcend the ego" all they want as other spiritual teachers recommend, but in the end it is not possible.

A capitalistic society will in fact take advantage of you if you "remove or transcend the ego." It is to your benefit to understand reality and the laws of human energy dynamics as outlined in this book. In the meantime, happy competing!

As I left the courthouse I noticed a figure racing after me. It was Darwin and he had gotten my attention:

Darwin said to me:

"Given the basic nature of natural selection, you are likely, sooner or later, to wind up with an intelligent species that's intelligent enough to reflect on itself and its environment. The kind of consciousness you are writing about in this book, Mr. Impersonal Energy, was essentially inevitable. You see, natural selection seems to be a process that by it's very nature builds vehicles for ever richer forms of consciousness. That alone is spiritually suggestive."

"One last thing," said Darwin.

"You're kind of like the new Buddha. He was born into great privilege, so he had a relatively easy time gratifying his desires. And by virtue of being born to privilege and what you now call your 'high energy/mass multi-categorical hybrid energy score sheet,' you may have experienced his same problem—gratifying desires much more easily than others. Then insufferable boredom set in. This is what in fact motivated you to write this book. My theory of natural selection holds. Because we have been built through natural selection, which is all about self-preservation and self-interest it actually makes sense that unhappiness or 'energy leakage/loss' as you put it is still consistent with Darwinian logic. "In fact," Darwin said, "happiness is something that is designed by natural selection to evaporate. It is designed not to last but to keep you motivated. If you imagine an animal that upon having sex says 'okay, I'm happy forever now,' that's an animal whose genes are going to lose out to a different animal that's says 'Wow, that was fun, when I become unhappy a little later on, Ill want to do it again, you know.' This is the reason why gratification is so fleeting."

As I left the courthouse I shook my head and smiled. I said to myself "that Darwin—he always did have to get the last laugh." Once Darwin was out of sight for good, I sat by a tree and meditated about what Darwin had said to me. In final analysis, Darwinian logic makes some sense but it simply is off the mark with regards to human beings and is not a spiritually suggestive outlook of life. #1 The goal of man is not survival (sorry Scientologists) and having offspring (sorry Darwinists). The goal of man is to selfishly relieve, reduce, avoid, or eliminate all forms of conceivable human suffering, which is why suicidal and self-destructive behavior occurs and will always occur. #2 to miss spirituality is to miss the essence of life. When Darwin talks about natural selection in "survival of the fittest" language and states that the strongest survive, propagate and therefore increase the strength of the species he seems to be judging organisms (humans in this case) as "fit" or "unfit" for survival. I have clearly stated in these writings that life is ultimately impersonal, ultimately impartial, and ultimately neutral. Therefore whatever path you are on is simply your path and does not make you more "fit" or "unfit" for anything. Kurt Cobain was "fit" to live here for a certain time period, as was JFK JR. Who said people who do not survive and have children were "unfit" for this planet. They were "fit" for a certain time period and fulfilled their assignments just like we are all doing. A baby that dies one second old lived a lifetime that cannot be judged as "fit" or "unfit" for survival. This was this baby's destiny, this baby's assignment. One thing will always lead to another in a trajectory that is no one's fault or everyone's fault. Ultimately, life is neutral. It is what it is and we all do the best we can every step of the way. To make this point clearer: If you end up in a mental hospital your whole life, end up committing suicide, end up dying on a military battlefield, or simply die very young (even one minute old), your path was your path and ultimately cannot be judged as "fit" or "unfit" for survival. Who made Darwin God and said "survival" was only for "fit" organisms? For all we know, not surviving is more "fit" because the organism could sense a perceived fairer exchange of its energy in another world we cannot yet comprehend. We are mere energy ball visitors (concealed by an earth suit that happens to made out of skin) to this planet doing the best we know how to do. In the ultimate end, we are all equal. A life cannot be judged as "fit" or "unfit" since we all have different energy assignments that we had no control over what we received, when or why in the first place. Since I am on a blind conditioned energy system assignment (like you are), I, at this moment **have no idea where this book is taking me or if ill even finish it.** But today I felt like writing so I am. I don't know why I was given it to write, but I was, so I am. The more I write, the more I feel it is a "do or die" situation and that I must do it. This is how everything gets done ultimately—"do or die." "Free will" being an illusion is a teaching you should review at this stage now (the gold key to life). If you don't agree with this book, then maybe it is your assignment to write your own book and refute me all you want.

Doorway Thirty-Nine of reality

Teaching: How to feel better part three

What is Energy imbalance disorder?

Energy deficit/leakage/loss disorder or Energy gain/infuse/implode disorder is a persistent pattern of unstable moods, intense and unstable relationships. One does not simply "leak or gain too much energy" all the time. When they acquire the equilibrium amount of energy that they feel they deserve in life, the feel better. This is the definition of a stable person—human energy equilibrium. Overall in societies, energy leakage/loss disorder, the energy imbalance on the "losing" side is much more common and is a slow depressing downhill slide. The inability to pay attention to people or things because the person perceives there is not enough "in it" for him/her.

What are the symptoms of Human Energy Imbalance disorder?

People with this disorder have some or all of the following symptoms:

- Unstable and intense relationships
- Impulsive acts with a high risk of harm, such as spending,

- sex, reckless driving, substance use, shoplifting, binge eating, or excessive showering or bathing
- Rapid shifts from a normal mood to depression, irritability or anxiety
- Inappropriate, intense anger or lack of control of anger, violence
- Suicide threats, thoughts, or behavior, or self-mutilation
- Persistent confusion with long-term goals or career choice, choice of friends, or values
- Chronic feelings of emptiness
- Frantic efforts to avoid real or imagined abandonment
- Enjoys spending time in psych wards and/or always feel a need to go there, however will want to leave as soon as insurance says they will no longer pay.
- react to criticism with feelings or rage, shame or humiliation
- take advantage of others to achieve own goals
- have a grandiose sense of self-importance. Note: They may in fact be "superior" because the multi-categorical score sheet is very strong and their perceptions may in fact be rooted in reality.
- hold a belief that his/her problems are unique and can only be understood by other special people
- have a preoccupation with fantasies of unlimited success, power, beauty, intelligence, or ideal love
- have unreasonable expectations of especially favorable treatment
- require constant attention and admiration
- be unable to recognize and experience how others feel
- be preoccupied with feelings of envy
- a belief that one is entitled to unlimited capital and those credit card debt/bills should simply go away and disappear. An attitude of "leave me alone, bother someone else to pay you" permeates the entitled person's mind.
- A "pass the buck" attitude of "don't bother me, just pay me and leave me alone."
- All is fun and games until the bill(s) arrive

What causes Energy Imbalance Disorder?

The cause is basically what all the theories of this book are about. There is ample evidence within the laws of physics that a) energy tends to condense before it releases; and b) all action has an equal and opposite reaction; and c) there is an inherent order in the Universe to everything, including people. Therefore what causes the "leakages" or "losses" or "gains" or "surges" are perceived unfair/unequal exchanges of human energy. In other words, paying attention to a person or thing without *enough* return on the attention investment. The person suffering subconsciously feels entitled to a perceived fair exchange of scarce, finite, ultimately impersonal, impartial, neutral human energy. They feel this right subconsciously because it was theirs (the energy) to begin with. This condition is not inherited. It is simply a matter of happiness = reality/expectations. Expectations then lead to entitlement for these expectations to be fulfilled. This person was raised a certain way and bred with energy inflows which condensed inside them. Then this person was released into the world as an adult and now subconsciously perceives that he/she is getting a perceived unfair exchange of energy consistent with his/her entitlement issues. I use the word "subconscious" instead of conscious because this condition is only now being made aware by this book. So once it's read and understood, the subconscious can now "awake" and become conscious or "aware." Other biological factors such as "brain chemistry" or a "chemical imbalance" may or may not be involved in these people, but these theories are NOT PROVABLE. It is the energy transaction FIRST which creates all moods and emotions. It is not provable if the energy transactions alter "brain chemistry," but it is easily understandable that it does affect the central nervous system. Other psychological factors are also involved for some patients. For example, having had childhood trauma (physical, sexual, or emotional abuse or neglect, or prolonged separation) could cause the patient to feel in "energy loss." This is because as human beings we are entitled to energy by our births and a certain minimum humane level of energy is expected.

This is our birthright. These people may feel "inferior" and "not understood" and need energy to simply feel better.

What happens to people who have Energy Imbalance Disorder?

The course of this illness is variable and often prolonged. The first serious symptoms often appear when one sees reality (such as this book) at the time of a significant loss of money, loss of physical beauty, or romantic break up. All patients with this disorder experience upheaval, chaos and pain. Sometimes the illness can be managed if and when the patient can find people who understand him or her. Understanding is Energy. A support group is needed with people suffering from the same exact disorder. Some patients require periodic brief hospitalizations when symptoms are intense. In the hospital, the patient is simply hunting for energy (subconsciously). If they have read this book, the search is now conscious. Other patients require longer inpatient treatment to provide safety while they are learning either to make their reality better (find more energy) or lower their expectations (entitlement feelings). Most patients should be able to make a reasonable work and social adjustment. Instability in relationships is inevitable as the ebb and flow of energy is normal and natural (who calls or emails who first, etc.), and depression is a frequent complication. Work functioning may be impaired by depressed mood, relationship problems, or the pursuit of goals which the person feels is "beneath or below" them. The patient is not able to connect to anything because in their view, there is simply not ENOUGH "in it" for him/her. The "potential energy" payoff is simply not enough. The person suffering NEEDS to balance scarce, finite, neutral HUMAN ENERGY to feel better.

How is Human Energy Imbalance Disorder Treated?

Treatment of **Human Energy Imbalance** disorder may include individual, group or family therapy, structure (making a daily written schedule so there are no long periods of unplanned time), support, medicines to relax the nervous system, limit-setting, consistent rules, education about the illness, social skills training, behavior modification and learning healthy communication and coping skills/relaxation techniques. Inpatient or day hospitalization may be necessary when symptoms make the patient a danger to self or others. The patient needs to go over category by category in meticulous detail the "multi-categorical" score sheet and sit down with someone who understands this condition to determine if their perceptions of themselves are accurate. If their entitlement issues are way off the mark then counseling in reality is needed. The counselor will have to say such things as "you're really not as attractive as you think you are," or "there is no evidence that you're as intelligent as you think you are." Inpatient or day hospitalization may be necessary *as long as doctors and family members understand this book. The cure for human energy imbalance disorder is of course to balance one's perceived entitled energy (there is a list of tiers in this book). Happiness = reality/expectations. This is true because the human nervous system gets conditioned (as all human systems do) and expects things due to prior conditioning (see Pavlov's Dog) in the "trial of reality" doorway.* What also helps is a belief in a higher power (religion etc). If you have too much energy—you need to release it). If you believe in this book, then you realize the "higher power" is neutral energy. Praying for neutral energy to make you feel better may help the condition. Go where your body tells you to.

What can I do to deal with my Energy Imbalance Disorder?

- Simply listen to your body *very carefully*. It holds all the truth. Go on your neutral assignment.
- Be patient with yourself as you attempt to recondition your nervous system (and all human energy systems).
- Trial and error for energy and body's reactions to the new external stimuli

- Develop methods to leave situations that are "beneath you." Simply pay attention to another who or what.
- Become aware of the reality that all people have different levels of energy and you can intuitively perceive that in your body's nervous system. The laws of physics as they pertain to energy are on *your side*. You are not crazy and what you are feeling is a normal survival defense mechanism. Your body can sense the energy loss/leakage.
- Find a satisfying job that is not "beneath you." Hold out until you get one that you feel there is enough "in it" for you (in your perception).
- Join an exclusive dating service or club.
- Work hard at being honest in therapy. If you feel superior, tell people that. Give them this book if you have to.
- Take medication if prescribed (to relax nervous system) only if the doctor you work with understands this book.
- Learn to express your feelings directly and appropriately. Use language such as "no offense, but I don't have the energy for this right now." Or "I cannot talk with you right now because I just don't have the "energy." Give the people around you this book so that they can understand your condition and your new language.
- Remember you can't always change the way you feel, but you can always try and change what you do about it. Simply STOP paying attention to the whom or what that is making you upset.
- Start your own support group for "energy loss/leakage disorder."
- Get a massage.
- Get around nature.
- Find understanding or any other form of energy.
- Do not pay when on a date just because it's the social norm (if you don't leave). If the other person is "beneath you" pay 50/50 and say it's just your policy.
- When on a date and miserable simply make up an excuse

and leave or make the person pay attention to you. Try to get "free therapy."
- Pay attention to the environment, not the person (if they are taking your energy) and you cannot leave.
- Learn ways to tolerate emotional distress. Distress usually rises to a peak quickly when you're hurt or upset, but if you tolerate the distress and do absolutely nothing about it, the pain will gradually diminish. Practice making no other response to emotional distress than to just tolerate it. Take a hot bath.
- Learn to fail. In other words, practice every day doing the things you find most difficult. Often the things we view as stupid are the things we find most difficult, so practice those things too. Learning that you can fail and survive is important.
- Play games with people who are better than you, so you can learn how to lose without severe distress.
- Identify the ways you put other people down. Ask other people to help you do this since it's often easier for other people to see your behavior clearly than for you to see your own. Once you know exactly how you put other people down, stop or keep doing it. Do whatever makes you feel better about yourself; just be aware of what you are doing.
- Become a happy, more accepting recluse/hermit
- Get a dog/cat or any pet since most people are "beneath you" in your perception and not worthy of your attention.
- Face the phone away from you and simply pretend you are listening to the person who is trying to attain your energy (attention). If you do not want to give it to them, then don't, but pretend you are by saying such things as "hmm I see." Then turn the phone away from you so you won't have to listen. The trick is to make the other person think you are listening.
- Understand that the "free" will as an illusion teaching is the most difficult lesson in life. Practice acting "as if" you

have it. Understanding that you are on an energy assignment and there is nothing you can do about except live the life you are meant to live. Be aware of your hunt for energy.

What happens if the symptoms return after I get them under control?

Certain life events are especially stressful for people with this illness and increase the risk of relapse: therapist's or other vacations; job demotion, worsening finances; loss of significant relationships especially loss of romantic love; birthdays, anniversary dates, and holidays; having a perceived "inferior person" talk down to you; discharge from a hospital or program; changes in physical health or beauty, including pregnancy, abortion, trauma or illness. If signs of relapse appear, there should be a specific plan decided in advance for actions that can be taken (e.g., brief hospitalization, medications for nerves, or relatives and immediate family should pay attention to you or give you more money!). There will be times when symptoms become more pronounced. These times are oftentimes of stress or anxiety and are called relapses. If signs of relapse appear, there should be a specific plan decided in advance for actions that can be taken (e.g., brief hospitalization, medication, increased structure, etc.). Make sure your doctor has a copy of this book and understands the provable laws of physics as they pertain to energy!

Quite simply, how to get better:

1. Buy this book
2. Talk about it
3. Become aware
4. Categorize yourself on the score chart (be honest)
5. Translate what the book says into your own personal life

with the goal of not losing or surging energy. Your goal is to have human energy equilibrium.
6. Find a passion or people who are worthy of your attention
7. Distract yourself (if possible) whenever you can (movies, etc.)
8. Write your own book and disagree with me all you want.

Where can I get more information about "human energy imbalance syndrome/disorder?"

This is the first book written in history bringing awareness to this problem.

www.truenatureofreality.com is the homepage of these revolutionary theories and philosophies.

Doorway Forty of reality

Teaching: "Good" and "Evil" are the passwords that open up the doorway of War

First of all, we must admit that the idea of a neutral God that created only neutral energy would not work if his name were evoked in a war between "good" and "evil." This is because if God is only neutral energy than who has the final say on who is "good" and who is "evil." Surely, if this book were to catch on, no Dictator or President would utter such nonsense to "rally the nation and troops" for a certain cause against an axis of "evil." "Evil" is clearly a matter of perspective as it relates to what is selfishly perceived "best" or not best for each individual's selfish conditioned nervous system (energy systems).

The War against Iraq

My "good" American God versus your "evil" Allah (God). Bush versus Hussein. It should be obvious now to you the reader after reading this book that all that is going on in reality is competition for scarce, finite, ***ultimately impersonal, ultimately impartial, ultimately neutral human energy***. The reason why everything is ***ultimately*** is because it was this way to begin with before mankind started judging and filtering everything through man made laws and rules—selfishly. The energy started out neutral, then goes through the filter that is mankind judging and labeling everything, and then ends up neutral again (the way it all started). Once again, God does not play dice or favorites. Period. This makes all conflict, stress, and anxiety in human beings inevitable however because there isn't enough of this energy to go around. The reason why the leaders of the world use the words "God" and "Allah" so much is because of Law #1. Religion is a very mobilizing weapon of mass destruction and we shall attack "in the name of God" and we will win this conflict "Godwilling." "God is on *our side*!" Bush, Blair, and Hussein are/were not aware people so they continue to believe in "good" versus "evil" instead of the much more sensible conflict over scarce, finite, ultimately impersonal, ultimately impartial, and ultimately neutral human energy. Once again, *there simply isn't enough to go around.* Aren't you people aware that nobody ever thinks of themselves as the evil ones in all this conflict? The 9/11 "terrorists" thought of themselves as heroes or "martyrs." *It's always the other guy who is evil, sick, and mad. We say this about others to us feel better about things that we cannot otherwise explain.*

Question: Why are the victims of September 11, 2001 heroes?
Answer: It makes us feel better to call them this. Since when does a hero sit at his desk and have a plane run into him? Anybody can do that and it doesn't take skill or anything to simply sit there and unknowingly have a plane crash into your office space. As far as the people who died trying to help—since when are heroes people who are/were conditioned on a certain trajectory in life to help other people and whose job and duty it is to help in such a crisis? This is what they have been trained to do their whole entire lives? Basically they are heroes because of the timing of their births to certain parents? If that is the case—every human being is a so-called "hero."

Back to the 9/11 terrorists

We simply pooh-pooh the terrorists as "evil people" who had "gone mad" instead of witnessing their ultimately neutral assignments play themselves out to their individual death vortexes. I will change my mind on the day that it can be proven to be that God/Creator/Whatever has a personality and cares one way or the other about anything here on earth. Until then, it is safe to assume the "Big Bang" released neutral energy that does not judge or care about human politics. All that happened when the "Big Bang" occurred was that esoteric universal laws for human behavior were established along with the physical ones we already know about. Don't get me wrong about the nature of war. If somebody is about to kill or harm you or you think they will, then of course your survival self-interest must conquer, kill or destroy them first. All I'm saying is that it has nothing to do with "good" versus "evil." Its just neutral energy we fight over and that is that.

Question: When one looks at the Universe/nature with all its colors and beauty, how can you actually say it's neutral? Isn't its obvious awesome beauty and vastness inherently beautiful and therefore "good?"

Answer: First of all why does "beautiful" equal "good?" Secondly, as human beings we have evolved by Law #1. This means, the ones who are surviving have a better chance of survival by attaining energy whenever they needed it, so have been conditioned to call the Universe "beautiful" and therefore tip the scale every so slightly to thinking the Universe is inherently a "good" Universe. There is no evidence in reality that suggests the Universe is on one side or the other. People we call "evil" or "bad people" do not think this about themselves. It is only your perspective of the threat they pose to your well being that conjures up your negative judgments of them. If the "evil" people all of a sudden gave you a flashlight during a blackout when you couldn't see anything, all of a sudden—they would be "good" people. I am asking you to be spiritually stable and consistent that's all. I'm sure some people will think I'm "evil" for writing this. These writings are in fact *ultimately* neutral as are you, the "beautiful" Universe, the 9/11 hijackers, and me.

Doorway Forty-One of reality

Teaching: Selfishness

All diagnosis and treatment in psychiatry, especially biological psychiatry, presupposes the existence of something called mental illness, also known as mental disease or mental disorder. In this book, I have put forward a theory; a hypothesis that I believe helps explains "mental illness." As of this writing, there are *no provable* biological abnormalities responsible for so-called mental illness, mental disease, or mental disorder. The idea of mental illness as a biological entity is easy to refute. A diagnosis should indicate the *root cause* of a mental disorder, and other than my theory remains unknown. Quite frankly, there is no evidence that any of the common psychological or psychiatric disorders have a genetic or biological component. My theories do not cover any known physical trauma to the brain or head. I am just refuting the faulty brain chemistry/chemical imbalance theory that's all for your everyday run of the mill diagnosed depression, manic-depression, stress, and anxiety type disorders.

It is sometimes argued that psychiatric drugs "cure" or stop the thinking, emotions, or behavior that is called mental illness proves the existence of biological causes of mental illness. This argument is easily refuted: Suppose someone was playing the trumpet and you didn't like him doing that. Suppose you forced or persuaded him to take a drug that disabled him so severely that he couldn't play the trumpet anymore. Would this prove his trumpet playing was caused by a biological abnormality that was cured by the drug? As senseless as this argument is, it is often made. Most, if not all, psychiatric drugs are neurotoxic, producing a greater or lesser degree of generalized neurological disability. So they do stop disliked behavior and may mentally disable a person enough he can no longer play the trumpet, feel angry, unhappy or "depressed." But calling this a "cure" is absurd. The psychiatric pills are also directly connected to the energy of the doctor. He or she has compassion and hope for you which is directly associated with what's in the pill. So if your energy is not balanced and take a pill, the placebo of the pill will still give you energy balancing you need by the very fact that the pill represents forms of energy (hope, understanding, you're not alone, there are many people like you and compassion etc.)

In reality, where I live, people are thought of as mentally ill only when their thinking, emotions, or behavior is contrary to what is considered acceptable, that is, when others feel *their energy equilibrium threatened by the "sick' patient*. The so-called healthy people dislike something about them so they call him or her all sorts of labels and names to fight for their human energy back. One way to show the absurdity of calling something a mental illness not because it is caused by a biological abnormality but only because we dislike it or disapprove of it is to look at how values differ from one culture to another and how values change over time.

Suicide

A cross-cultural example is suicide. In many countries, such as the United States and Great Britain, a person who commits suicide or attempts to do so or even thinks about it seriously is considered "mentally ill." However, this has not always been true throughout human history, nor is it true today in all cultures around the world today. Probably the best-known examples of societies where suicide is socially acceptable are Japan and fundamentalist Islam. Rather than thinking of suicide, or "harakiri" as the Japanese call it, as almost always caused by a mental disease or illness, the Japanese in some circumstances consider suicide the normal, socially acceptable thing to do, such as when one "loses face" or is humiliated by some sort of failure. Another example of this would be the kamikaze pilots Japan used against the US or the present-day "martyrs" of the holy Islamic war (jihad). The World Trade Center episode of September 11, 2001 (suicidal hijackers) is another indication of different values for different cultures. Were the hijackers mentally ill? If so, who is the ultimate judge of that?

The reason for this is different attitudes about suicide and is in fact a "culture clash." In such places as Japan, and certain Arab cultures suicide is a perfectly acceptable way to go. Could it be that suicide is committed only by people with psychiatric illnesses in America and yet be performed by "normal" persons in Japan, Saudi Arabia, Iraq, Afghanistan, wherever, etc.? I think not.

The real issue is selfishness and is law #1 of reality. This is why I have repeated it so many times in this book. What is so wrong about admitting we are selfish creatures? *That is the mystery here that needs to be solved!*

When we don't understand the real reasons behind another person's actions (hint: selfishness to not suffer), we create myths to provide an explanation such as "evil." I'm sure you get the point now of what I've been driving at. Anyway, quite simply (and now I'm beating a dead horse), it's all about the selfish competition for scarce, finite, ultimately impersonal, ultimately impartial, and ultimately neutral human energy. Wars, murders, and killings, will still happen because the competition for this prized precious resource is fierce. This is an inevitable, normal part of human existence. All that needs to happen now so that societies can awake is to use the correct language. If Bush/Blair were enlightened they would say: "Our great nations are collectively suffering from energy imbalance syndrome with regards to the nation of Iraq. We feel an energy loss with regards to Iraq and we desire energy equilibrium once again. I/we understand good and evil is a matter of perspective and we do not believe or think we are the judges of what is "good" for other nations or not. All wars are inevitable because there isn't enough energy to go around, and we have an inherent right as selfish human beings to avoid, relieve, reduce, and eliminate all forms of psychological, emotional and otherwise conceivable human suffering as much as humanly possible. Since energy imbalance syndrome (getting a perceived unequal exchange of energy) is so undesirable, we are entitled to try and relieve ourselves of this horrible human condition. This is the defensive, protective, selfish nature of mankind and there is nothing we can do to change this truth. I, of course agree to Law #1."

Law #1

One last real world example:
The World Trade Center landlord is currently suing Cantor Fitzgerald for the back rent the firm owes from the time period Aug 1-September 10, 2001. Cantor Fitzgerald lost 685 human beings in the destruction.

Question: Do you blame the landlord?
Answer: No matter how insensitive you think this may be, *he is entitled to it*. This is because his mortgage company needs their money and the bank theirs. Nobody really cares *ultimately* how many people this firm lost. All they want is their entitled ultimately impersonal energy (in this case back rent otherwise known as money). Not one entity is willing to take the hit for this tragic and unexpected loss because energy is so precious, so scarce, and so difficult to attain.

Law #1—All human thought and action (including this book) has evolved to be one hundred percent defensive, protective, selfish, and self-serving so that one can avoid, relieve, reduce, or completely eliminate all forms of suffering via a perceived equal and fair exchange of energy. Overall human energy balance (equilibrium) is what we seek and deserve. Human energy imbalance is the ***root cause*** of all conceivable forms of human suffering and ***all mental illnesses.***

Happy Competing for Energy!

Epilogue

There are very common and frequent assignments, rare assignments (like this book), and everything in between. Each assignment has a different amount of energy (vibration or frequency) associated with it and this is why some people have more power and influence than others. In totality, the Universe is impersonal, impartial, and neutral although we experience "trial and error," positive and negative, "personal" energy reactions to the diverse energy interacting with our conditioned nervous and overall human energy systems as we go through our days and lives. It is important to understand that these "personal" energy experiences are solely based on our perspectives as it relates to our selfish, defensive, and protective conditioned human energy systems which only wants to avoid, relieve, reduce, or eliminate all forms of conceivable human suffering (psychological, emotional, existential etc.). The **SELF-PRESERVATION,** self-gratifying, masturbatory, defensive, selfish inherent nature of reality explains how and why every ultimately impersonal and ultimately impartial assignment gets done. Each person simply goes on a one thing leads to another karmic stream of condensing and releasing energy in a manner that will not be "more than a perceived fair exchange" because that equals guilt, or "less than a perceived fair exchange" because that equals resentment and pain. People simply desire to get what they feel entitled to, want they life they feel they "signed up for" and all the problems of humanity revolve around the simple fact that many times in life two or more human beings (living creatures in nature fight for food and territory) feel entitled to the same exact thing (human energy). There simply isn't enough to go around to satisfy everyone's entitlement for what they perceive they deserve.

Happiness = Reality/Expectations

Parents must understand human energy conditioning (especially the nervous system), and must be held responsible for establishing a child's expectations for his or her life. If a child expects something—it must be due to ingrained conditioning. There is no other way for anybody to expect anything unless they had experienced the same cause and effect harmony/payoff previously

Question: Is this book "good" for humanity?
Answer: The human species is an evolving one and consciousness (awareness) of reality was/is inevitable. Ultimately, all of the Universe's assignments (this book is obviously one of them) are impersonal, impartial, and neutral. All this book offers is evolution of the species with regards to consciousness. It is a *new and different* way of looking at reality, not "better" or "worse." It is what it is—*ultimately* neutral.

Quick Review

Question: Are you are aware that just about all your teachings are exactly the opposite of what other spiritual teachers and doctors teach?
Answer: Yes I do. I believe all other philosophies and theories about reality are off the mark. I believe the entire psychiatric industry needs to be overhauled with regards to reality. I believe all spiritual teachers are incorrect and prior philosophies of reality such as Scientology simply miss the boat.

Spiritual Teachers Refuted

1) They say: "all is one." I say: "all has an order." In nature (wild kingdom) there is a "food chain." In humans, there is a hierarchical structure to how much energy each of us has (multi-categorical score-sheet)
2) They say: "be selfless." I say: "be selfish and selflessness does not exist anyway. The true nature of reality is based on the selfish desire to relieve, avoid, remove, or eliminate all forms of conceivable human suffering at all costs. Even the martyr isn't a martyr. Psychology (feelings) is *always* behind it."
3) They say: "remove and transcend the fears and desires of the ego." I say: "that's not possible and a capitalistic society will take advantage of you if you could anyway. It's all about energy and energy in = energy out."
4) They say: "perception isn't reality." I say: "perception is reality."
5) They say: "there's enough for everyone to get along." I say: "life is a fierce and brutal competition for energy. Conflict and clashing entitlement feelings for energy is normal and inevitable."
6) They say: "free will exists. Therefore there is good and evil." I say: "free will is an illusion and there is no ultimate judge of good and evil. There are just blind "trial and error" conditioned energy system assignments or energy assignments."
7) They say: "the Bible or other scriptures say this and that." I say: "the Bible etc. is not provable scientifically. All religious scriptures fall under Law #1 because all of reality does and it is inescapable. Religious scriptures claiming one miracle after another is simply Law #1. The Noah's Arc claim in Turkey, the miracles Jesus performed etc. are still not scientifically provable and never will be. Face it. They will forever remain theories. My theories are *less outlandish.*

Doctors Refuted

6) They say: "Psychosis exists." I say: "Psychosis is a perspective."
7) They say: "chemical imbalances and/or brain chemistry problems are the **root cause** of mental illness." I say: "unequal energy exchanges are the **root cause** of mood and emotional problems. The chemistry part may or may not be true, but the **root cause** is the energy exchange that may or may not alter chemistry. It is the energy exchange first. Psychiatric drugs for the nervous system do in fact work, but the brain chemistry/chemical imbalance altering drugs remain an improvable theory at best. "The exact mechanism of how they work remains unknown" is what the psychiatrist always says. My theories are in fact *less outlandish*

Final Comments

If you do remove or transcend the ego and feel okay living that way—then that's great for you—you've found your path. But you must be aware that you have removed yourself from reality because reality is inherently competitive by its very nature. Someone else will get what you deserve because you have surrendered to law #1 with the "I didn't want it anyway excuse/defense." Once again, if this is your path, you still will always be adhering to law #1. There is no escape from it.

Enlightenment and "removing/transcending the ego"

Your version of enlightenment is different than mine. Yours welcomes poverty and your leader is not I. I'm sure if I were to go out to dinner with your leader however, a squabble would take place when I unexpectedly refused to pay for my fair share of the meal. I will say, "why do you care if you pay for me, you don't have an ego remember—you've removed and transcended it?"

Enlightenment, **like everything on earth, is in the eyes of the beholder.** *It just means awareness.* Become aware of Entitlement and through your awareness of this one word, you will become "Enlightened"

Epilogue Continued

Teaching: Free Flow Thoughts

I wish I could find some sort of meaning in this life other than survival through these writings. Well if this is my path to write this then so be it. The free will question—well it is what it is and was well discussed in one of the doorways. I call it a grand illusion, a hoax. I did not choose to write this freely, I was forced to by the Universe or I wouldn't have felt right not writing this book. Man is nothing but a complex super duper robot trying to selfishly survive as long as the suffering is not greater than the will to live. Life and survival is "good" and "more fit" while non-survival is more "unfit," "bad," and "evil." Who said so? Why is that a law? Where is it written? The Spiritual Writings say so? Why are there so many different views of who has it "right" and who has it "wrong" with regards to "Holy Scriptures." Why does everyone think the other person/nation is crazy or evil when involved in a conflict with him or her? Who knows what is good or bad? Did the Messiah say so? Who made *insert any name you want here* the Messiah and the *ultimate authority* on everything? I think not. Listen to your body on your blind *ultimately neutral*, *ultimately impersonal*, and *ultimately impartial* assignment and be amazed to see what is in store for you as you chase a perceived fair exchange with God—neutral impersonal impartial energy.

Meditation on options is a good idea so that you can feel your body react to them and your inevitable path will flow.

What is "self destructive" behavior anyway? It's in the eyes of the beholder but is considered to be when the organism starts to die a slow death. Why would someone be self-destructive?

Answer: People want to feel good and the short-term gain versus long-term loss is in the favor of the net effect of the short term balancing (feeling good). Everything a person does, says, or thinks, is judged solely on how much overall human suffering it generates for the selfish person in question. Feeling good maybe self destructive in the long run and this is how we know that "just survival" as the goal of man is simply not true. Many human beings "choose" not to survive. Call them insane, call them what you want as long as you understand you call them these name because you adhere to Law #1 of the Universe.

The goal of man is Law #1.

Law #1—All human thought and action (including this book) has evolved to be one hundred percent defensive, protective, selfish, and self-serving so that one can avoid, relieve, reduce, or completely eliminate all forms of suffering via a perceived equal and fair exchange of energy. Overall human energy balance (equilibrium) is what we seek and deserve. Human energy imbalance is the ***root cause*** of all conceivable forms of human suffering and ***all mental illnesses.***

Printed in the United States
35824LVS00002B/85-87